COLLECTORS' SERIES

MASTERS OF THE DARK ART

VOL. 3: JOSHUA WERNER

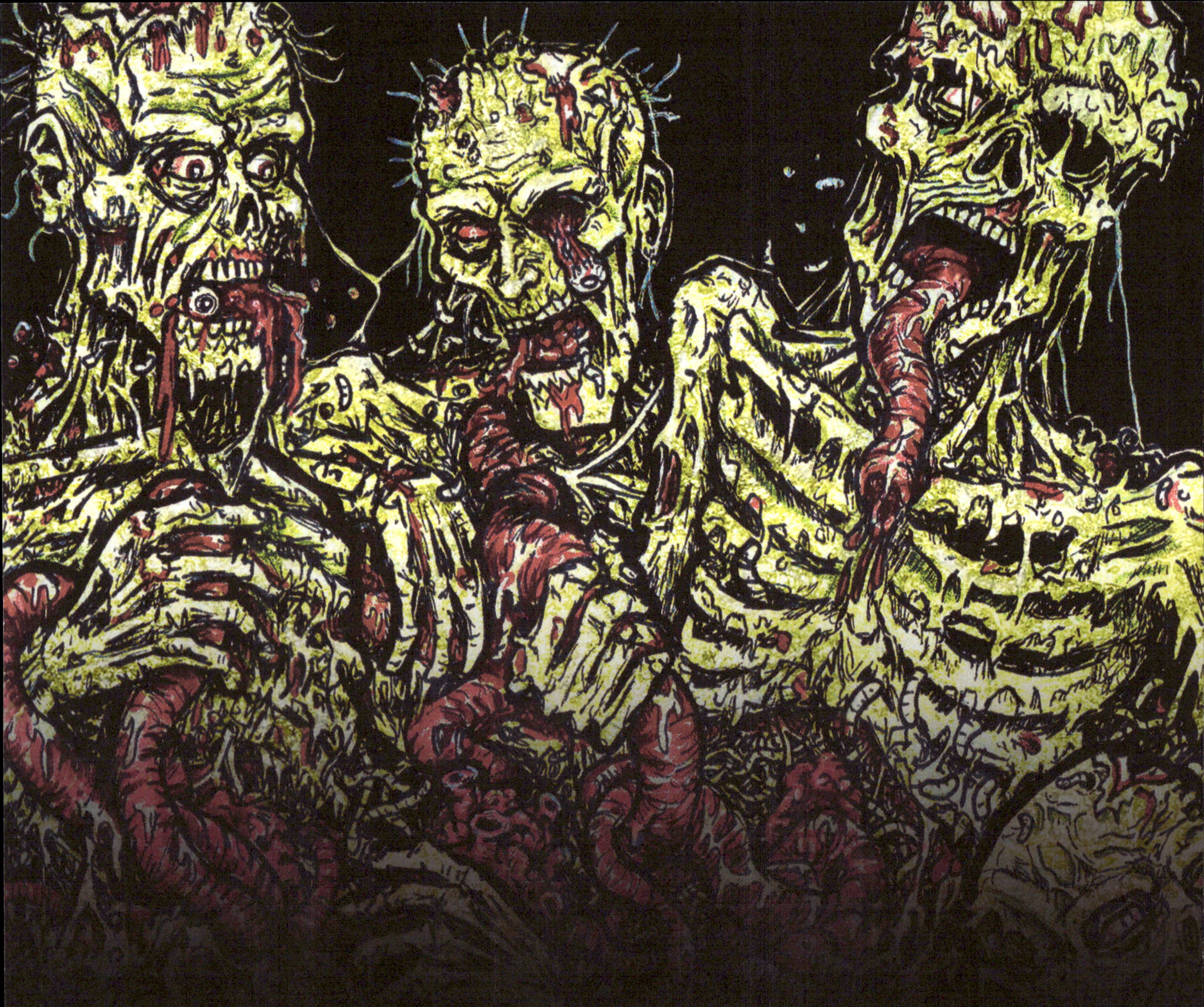

ARTWORK BY JOSHUA WERNER
EDITED BY PAUL BURKE

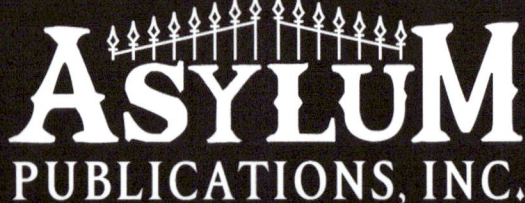

Distributed by **Binary** PUBLICATIONS

CEO AND EDITOR IN CHIEF PAUL BURKE
CREATIVE DIRECTOR JOSHUA WERNER

ISBN: 978-1-7339309-6-3
Masters of the Dark Art Vol. 3: Joshua Werner™. Published by Asylum Publications, Inc.™ All images are © by Joshua Werner. Asylum Pulications, Inc.™ and Masters of the Dark Art™ areTM 2019. All rights reserved. No portion of this publication may be reproduced or transmitted, in any form by any means, without written consent from the Publisher, except for any small excerpts for the purpose of review. For further information regarding custom photo/art books, ordering wholesale, or other inquiries, please write to asylumpublications75@gmail.com.

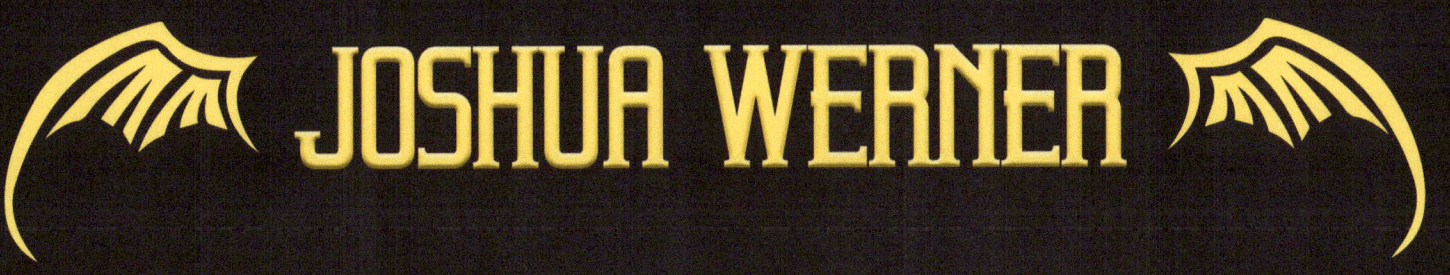

JOSHUA WERNER

Joshua Werner is an artist, author, actor, and designer based in Michigan. His vast body of work in the horror genre includes art for books, comics, trading cards, movies, and t-shirts. In addition to his career in freelance illustration, he's written stories and books in the horror genre and has produced and acted in horror films. He is also the Co-Founder of Source Point Press, a publishing company working largely in the world of horror.

His artwork covers several mediums, including oils, ink, gouache, watercolor, mixed media, and digital. His love for classic horror films continues to influence his work at every stage of his career.

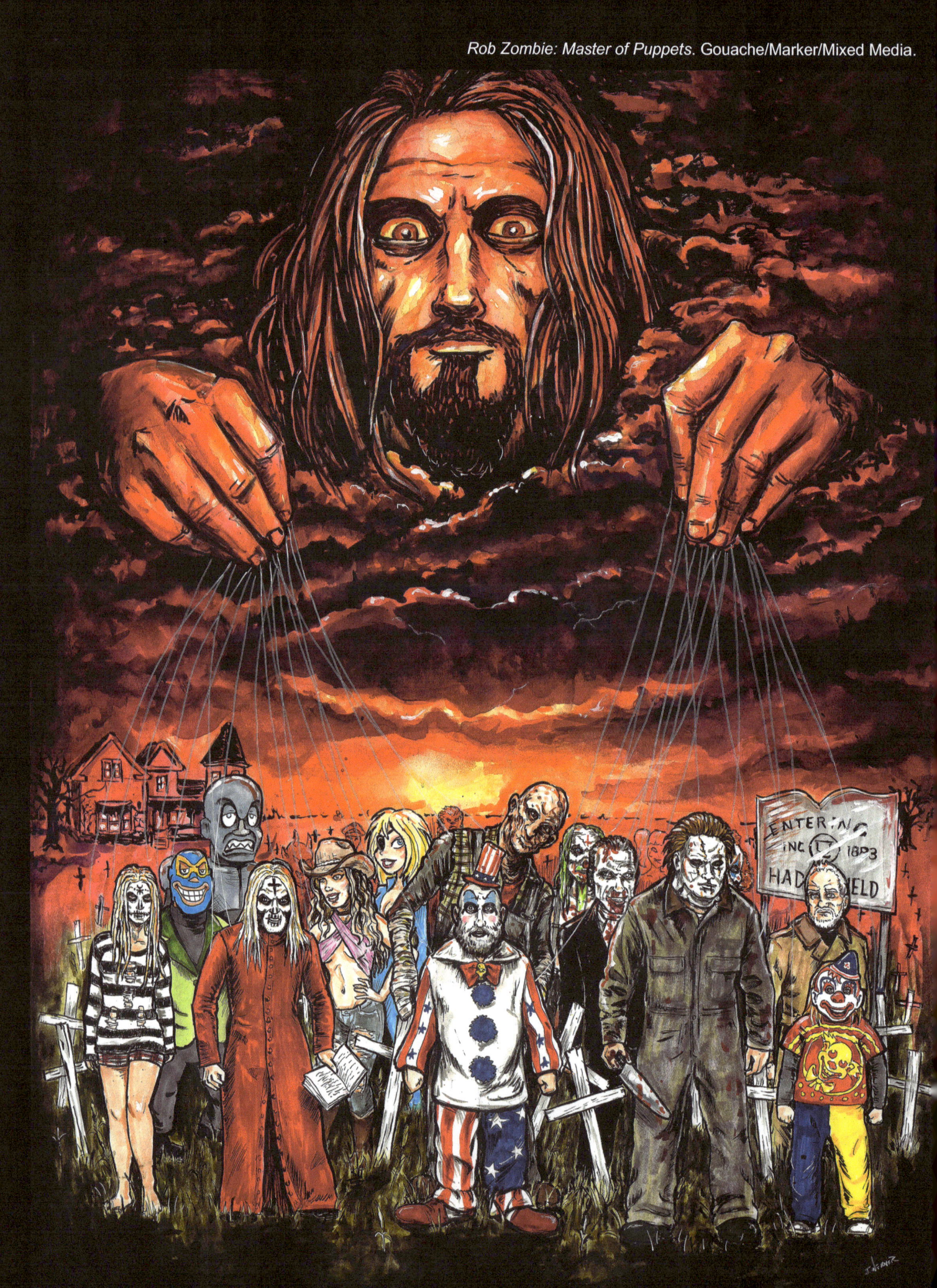
Rob Zombie: Master of Puppets. Gouache/Marker/Mixed Media.

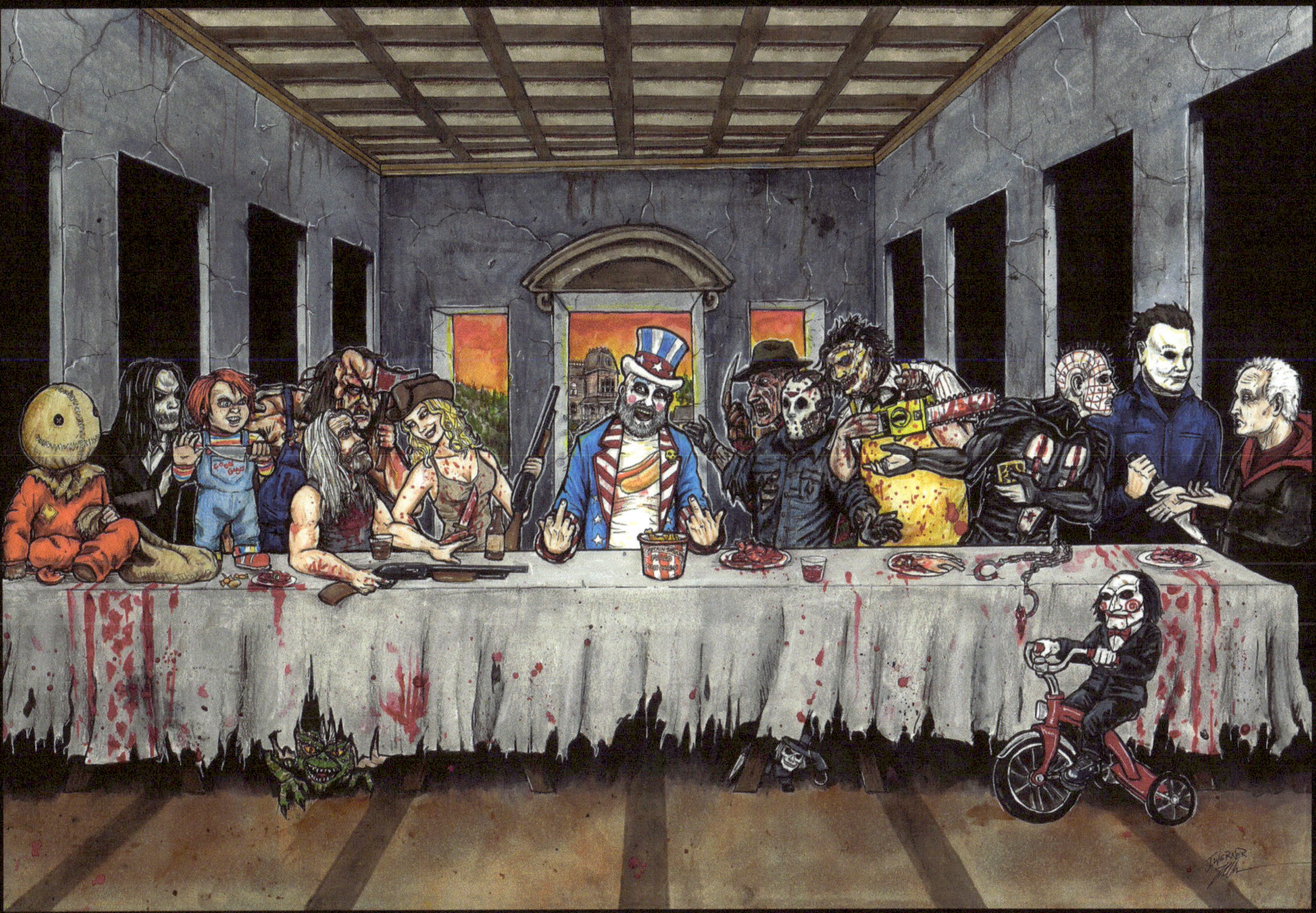

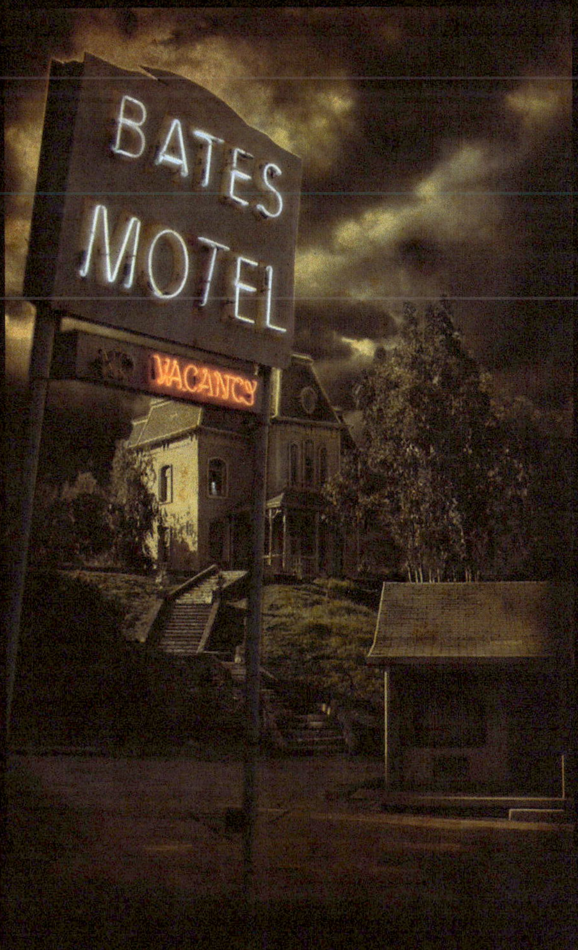

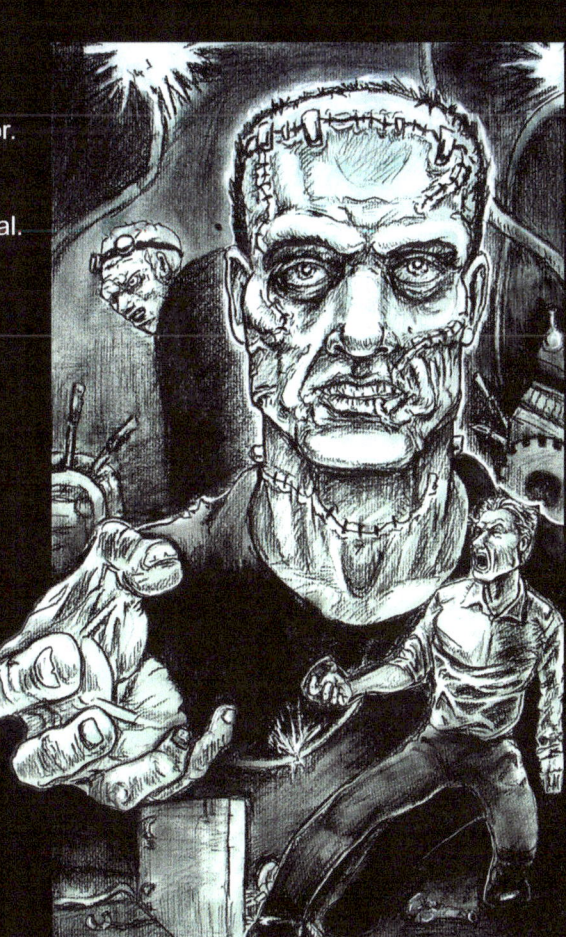

Above: The Last Horror. Mixed media.

Left: Bates Motel. Digital.

Right: The Monster Escapes. Charcoal.

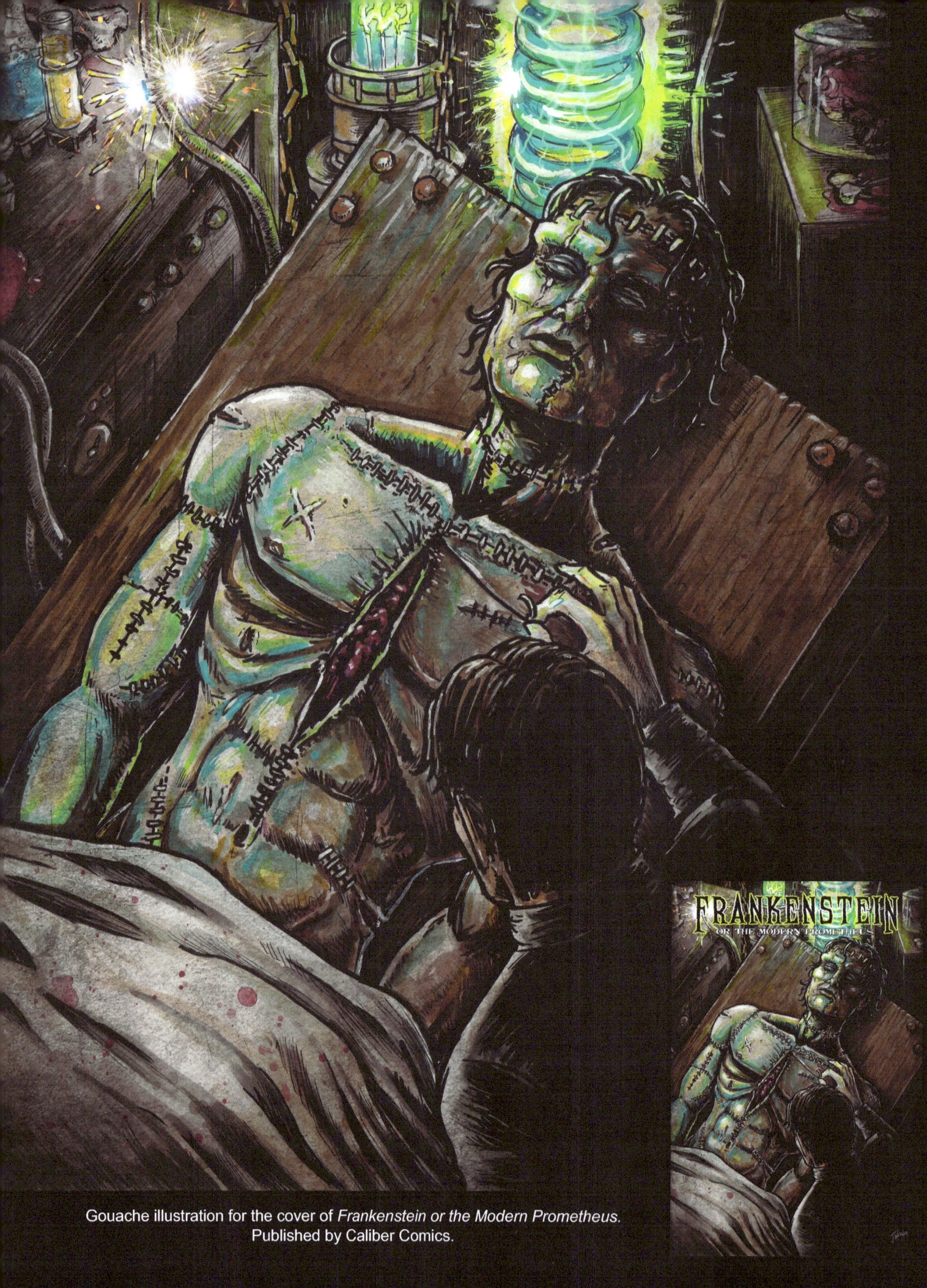

Gouache illustration for the cover of *Frankenstein or the Modern Prometheus*. Published by Caliber Comics.

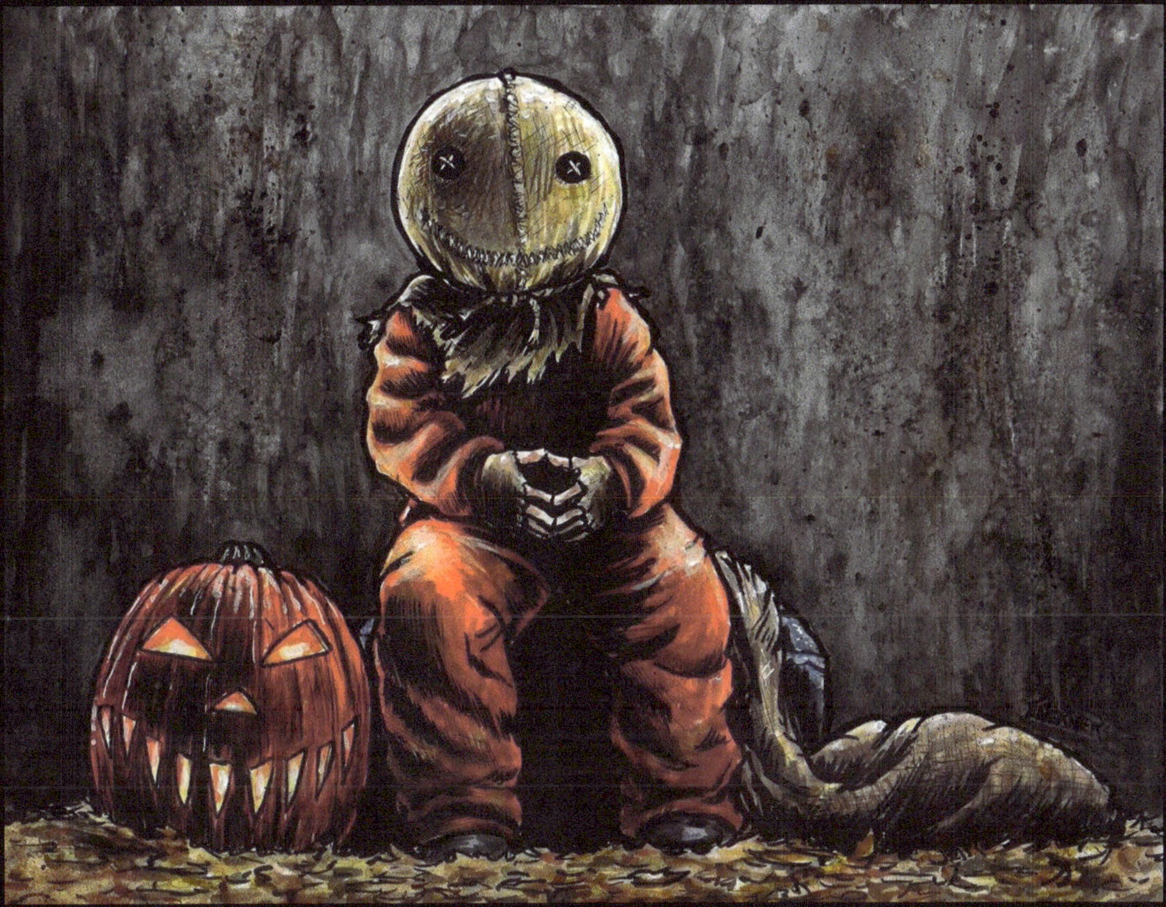

Above and below left: Trick 'R Treat commissions. Watercolor/Goauche/Marker/Ink.
Below right: My cover art and design for the novel Cannibal Fat Camp.

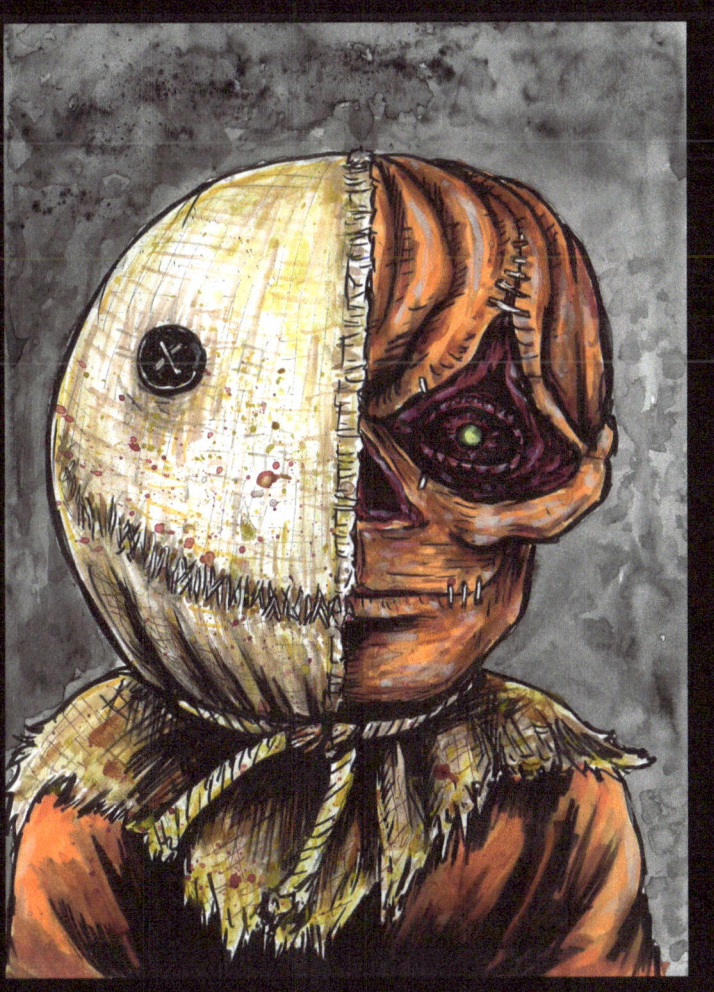
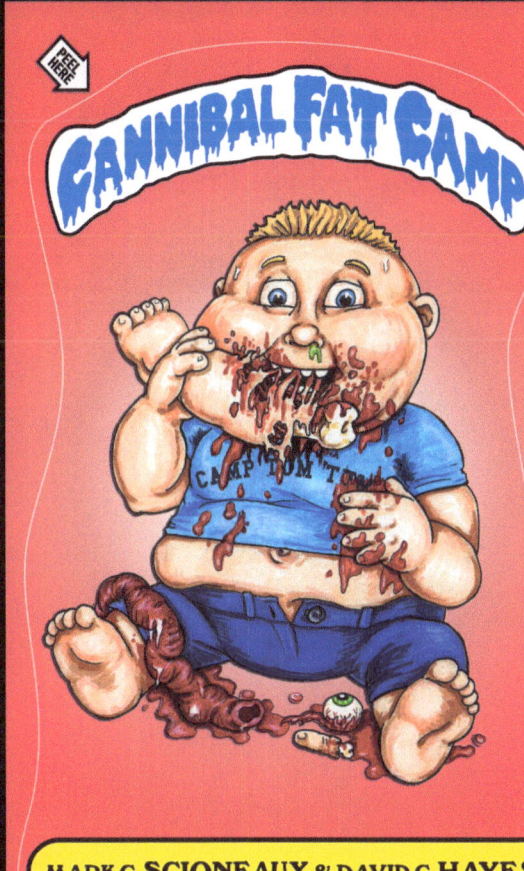

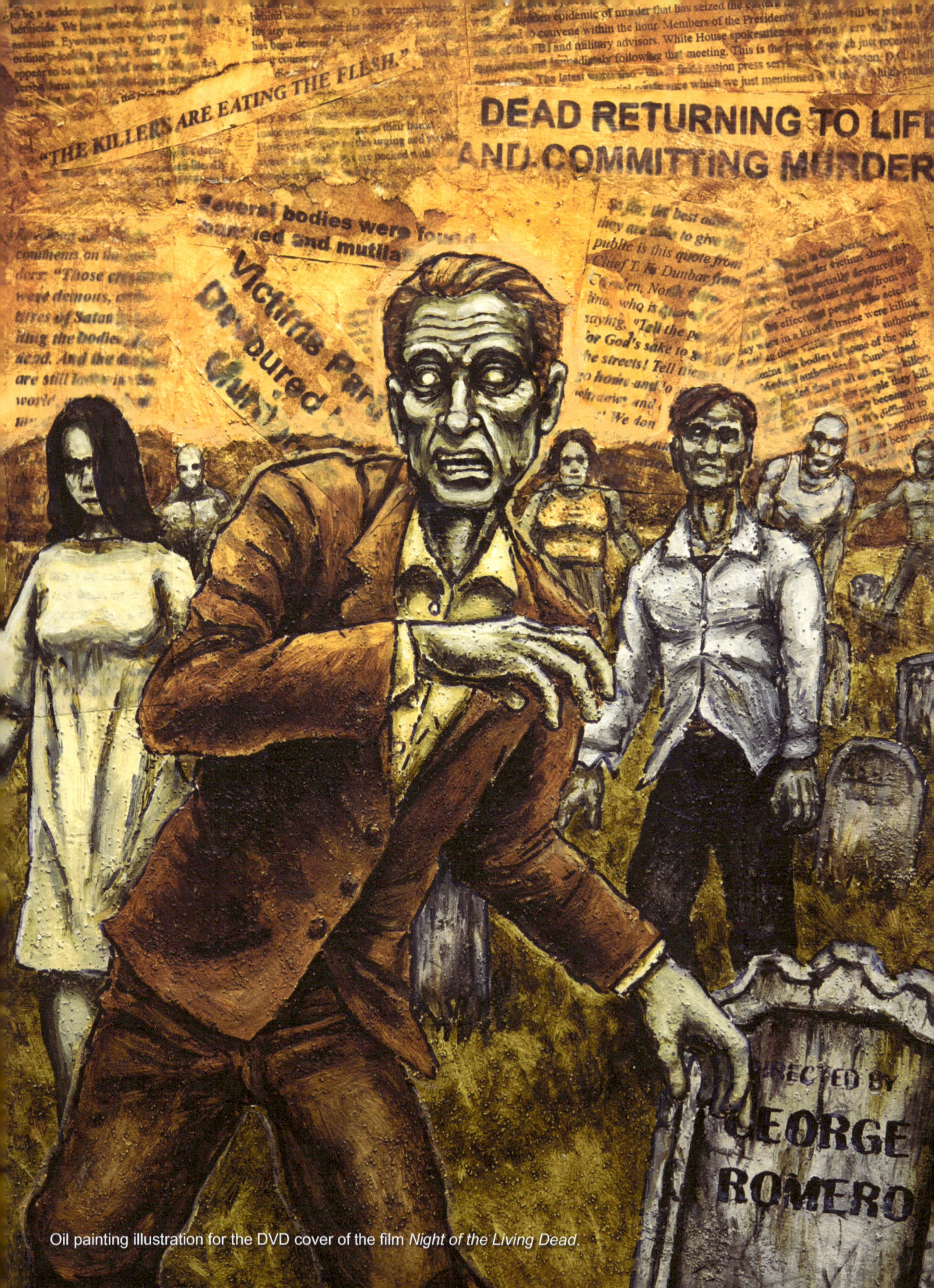

Oil painting illustration for the DVD cover of the film *Night of the Living Dead*.

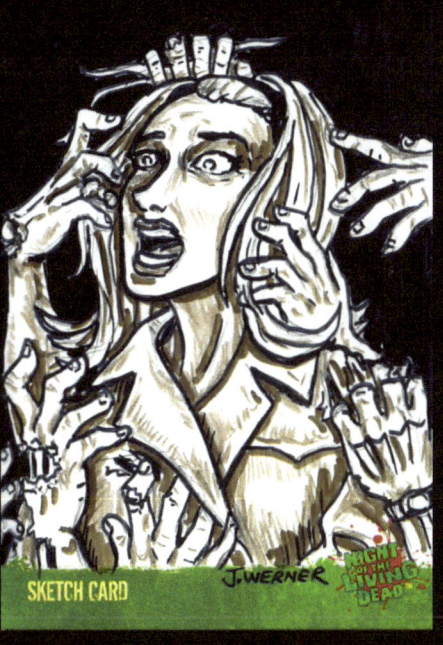 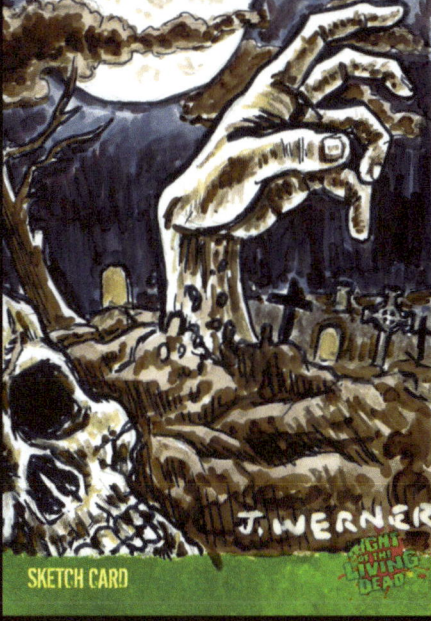 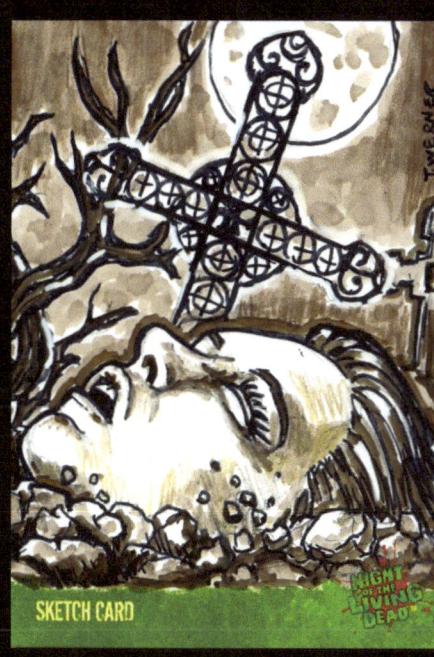
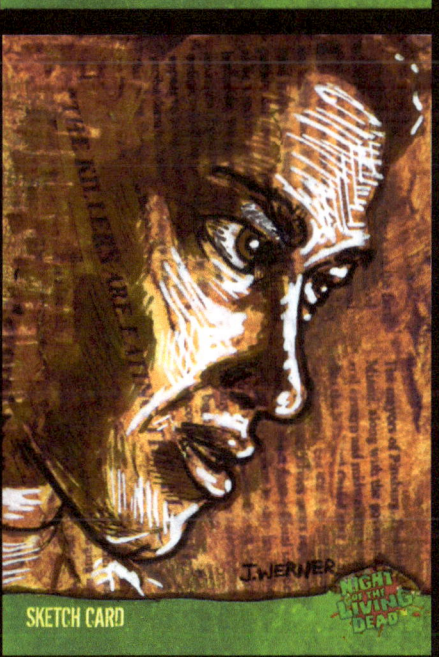 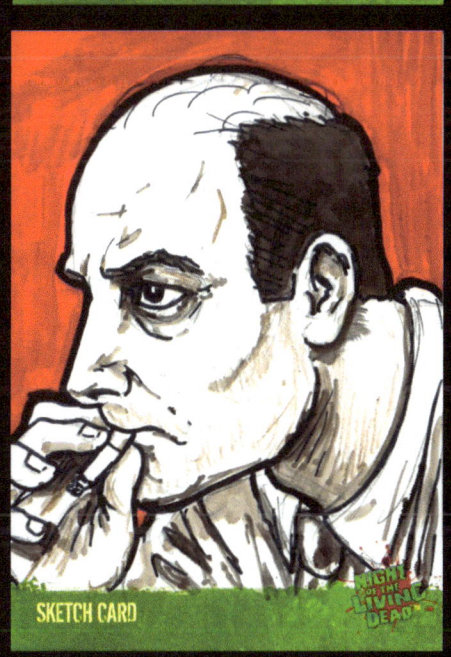 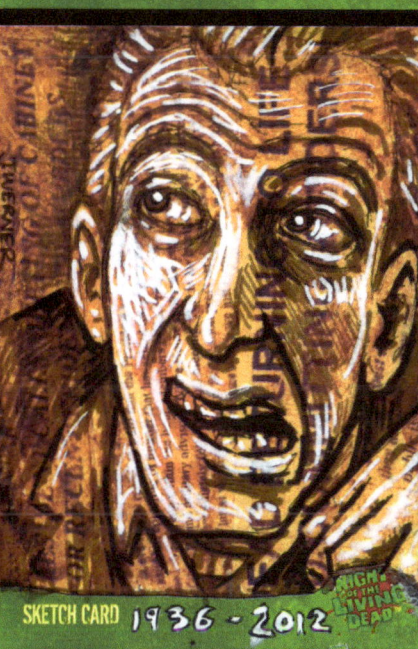
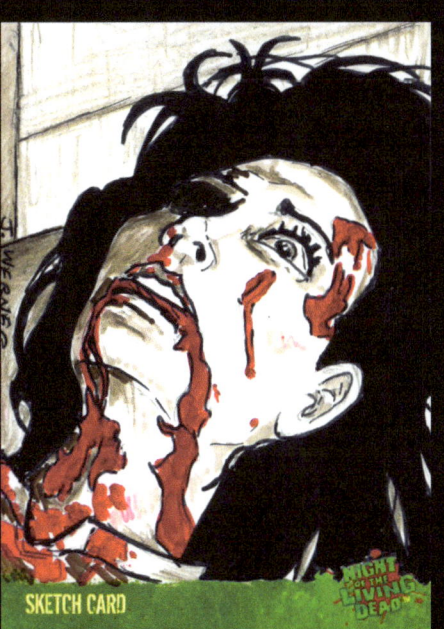 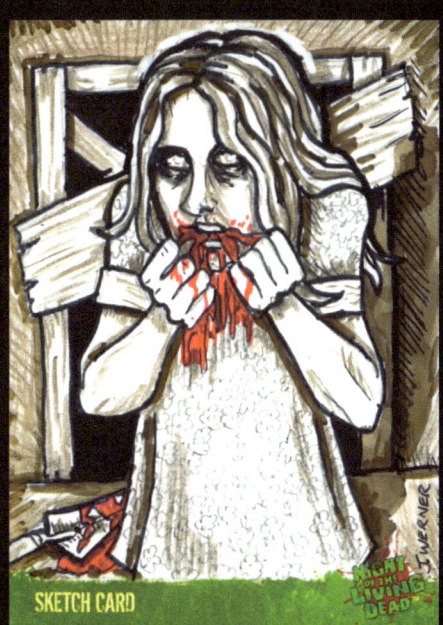 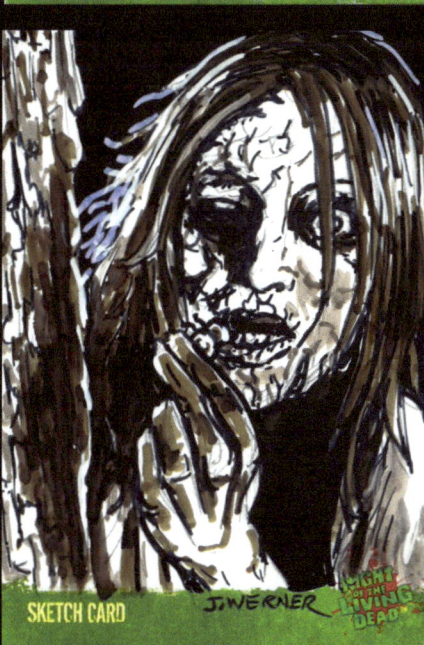

A few of my sketches for the *Night of the Living Dead* trading card set from Unstoppable Cards.

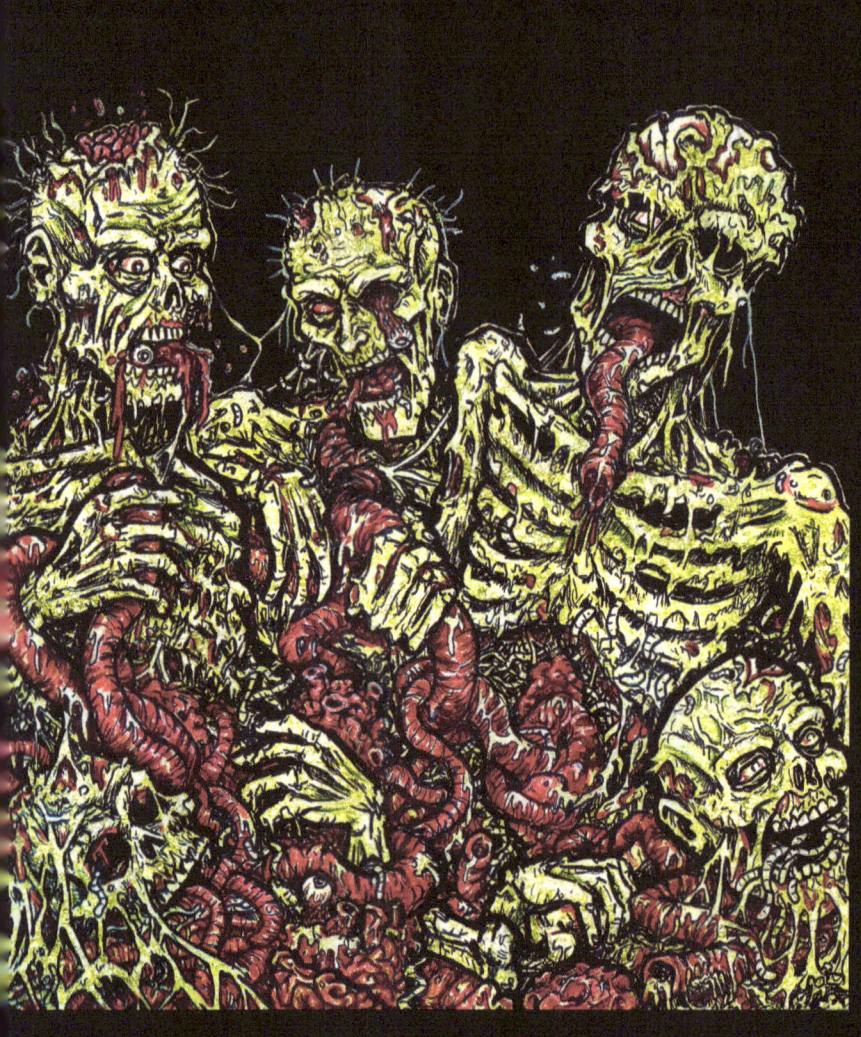
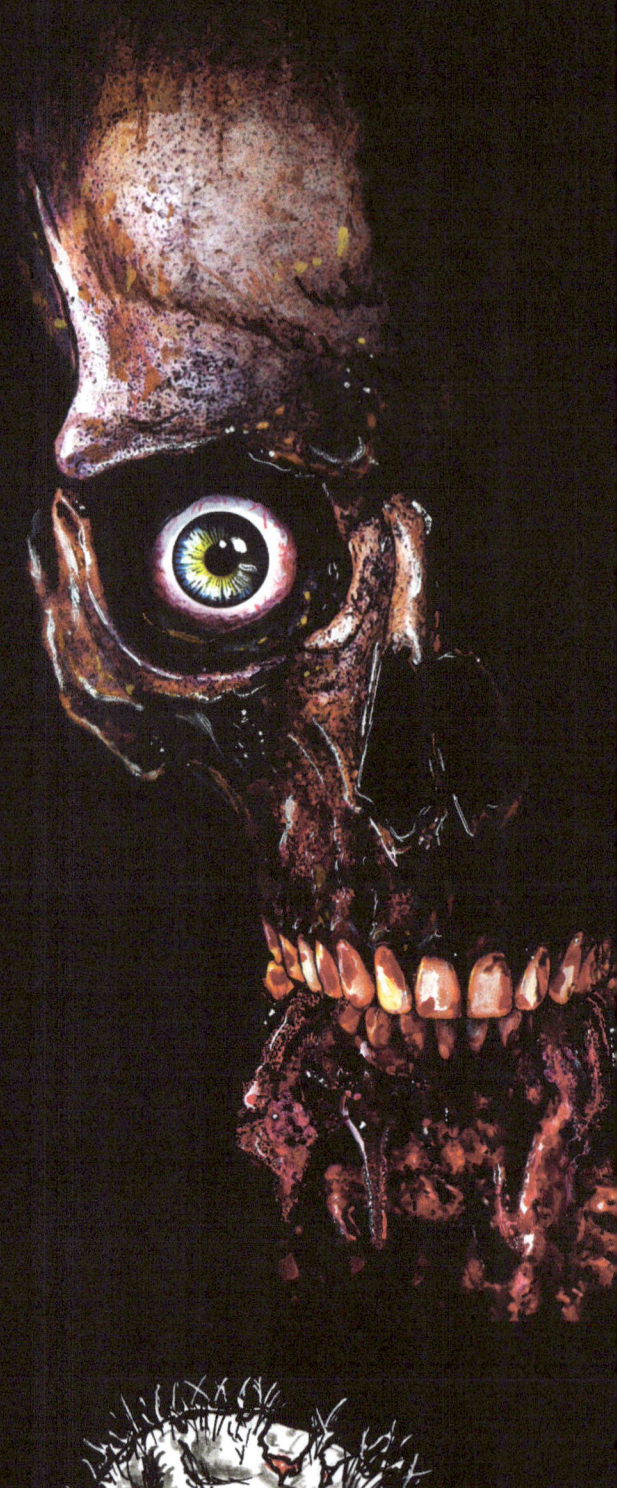
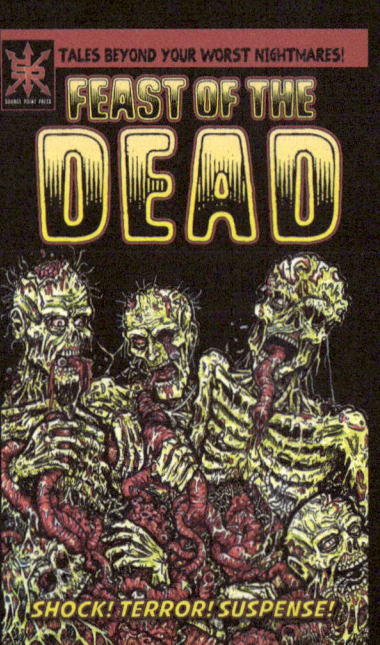
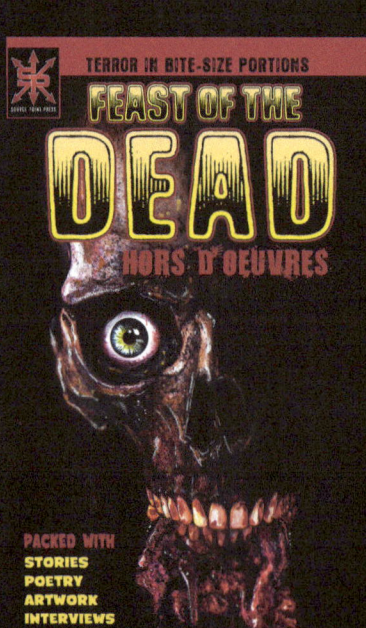
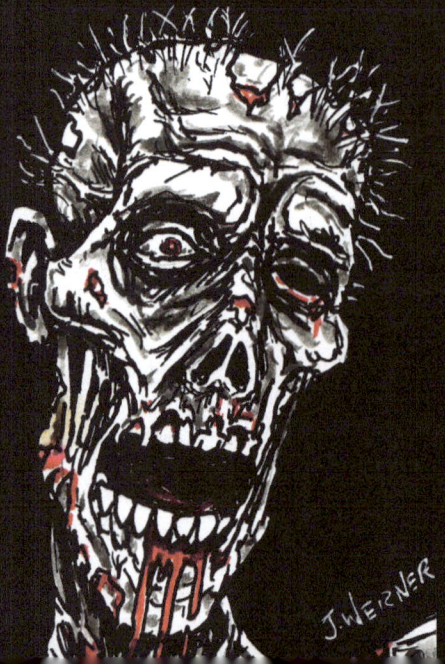

Above: Illustrations for the covers of *Feast of the Dead* and *Feast of the Dead: Hors D'oeuvres*. Mixed media. Published by Source Point Press.
Right: Zombie sketch card. Markers.

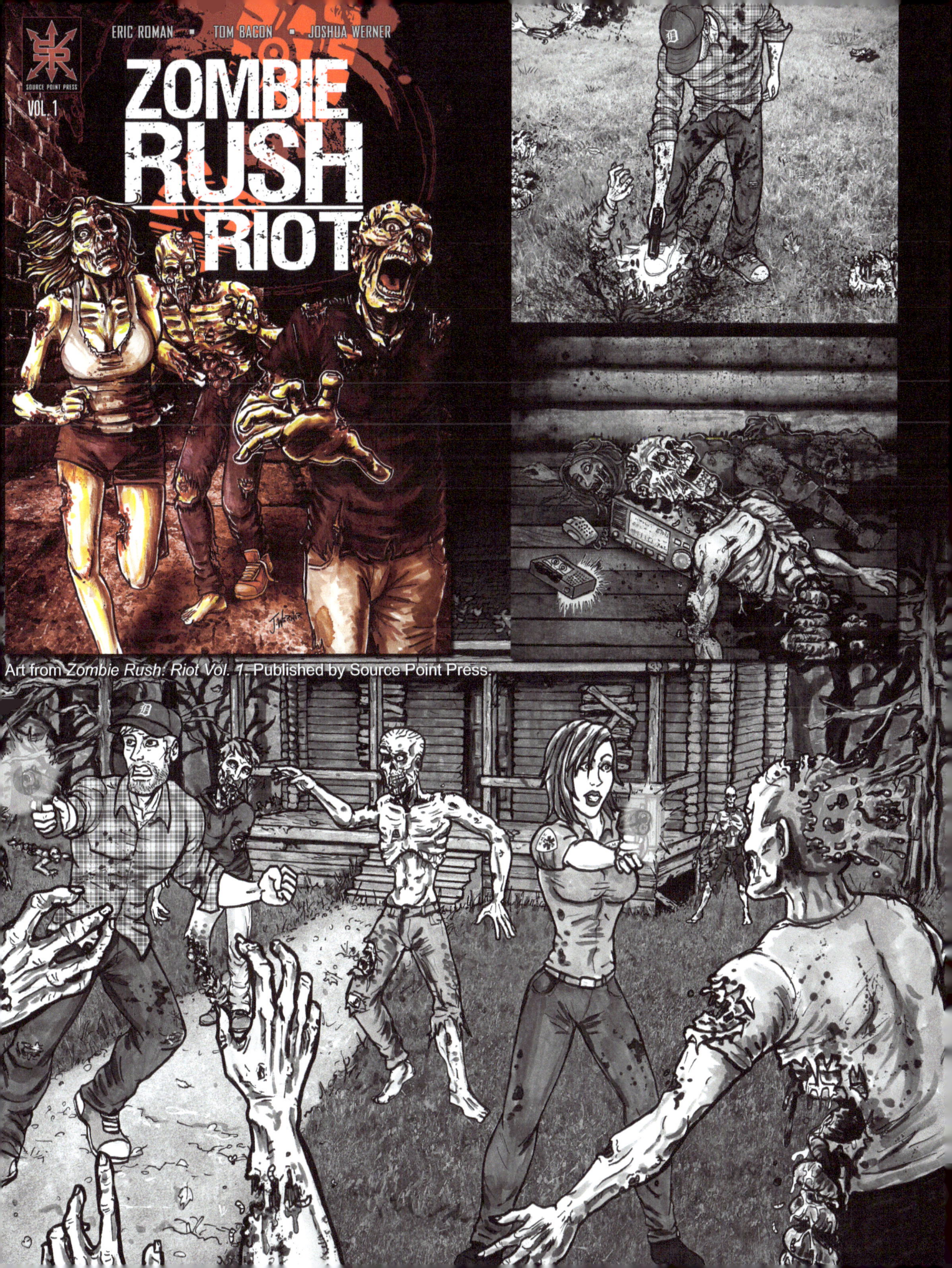
Art from *Zombie Rush: Riot Vol. 1* Published by Source Point Press.

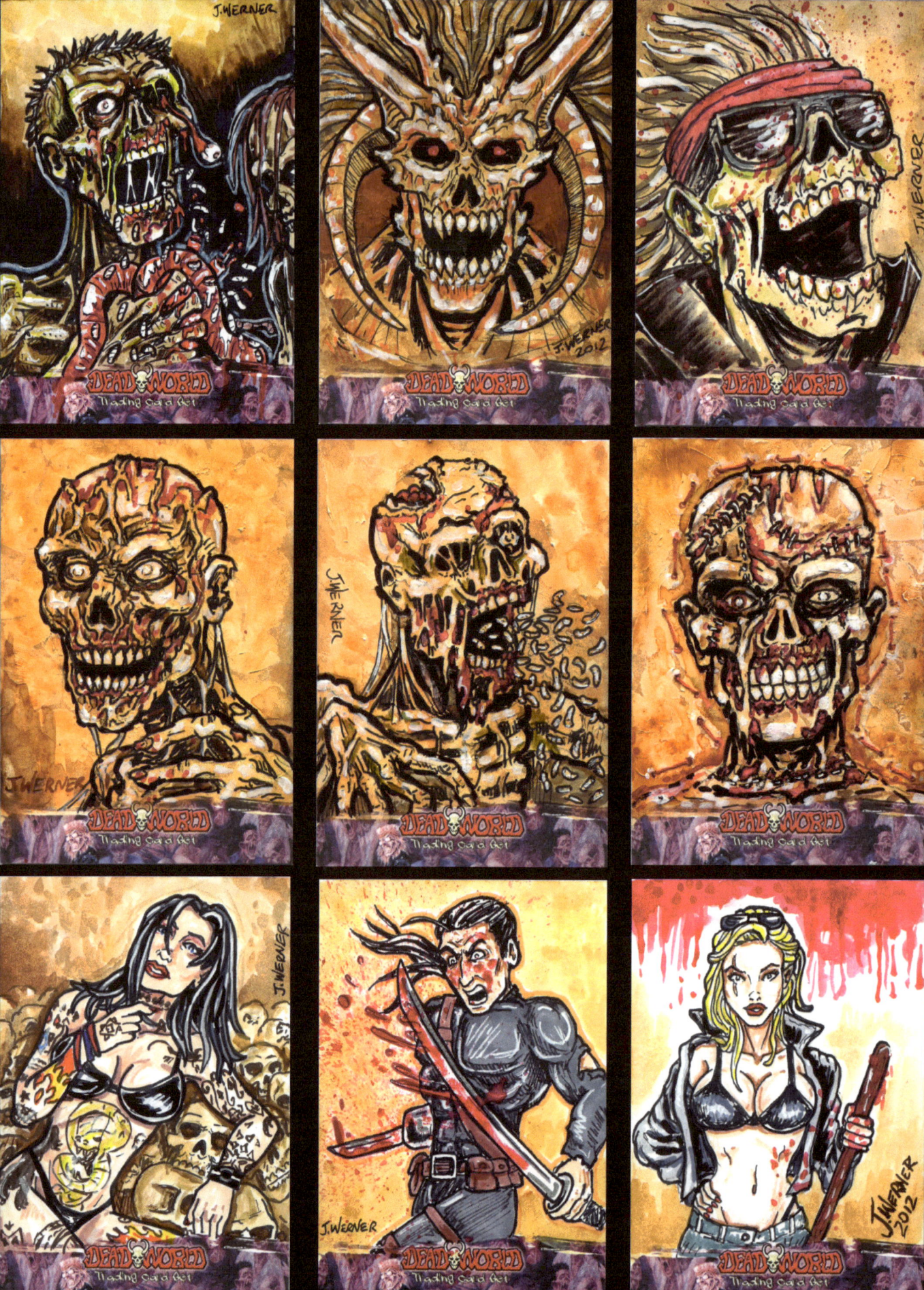

A few of my sketches for the *Deadworld* trading card set from Breygent.

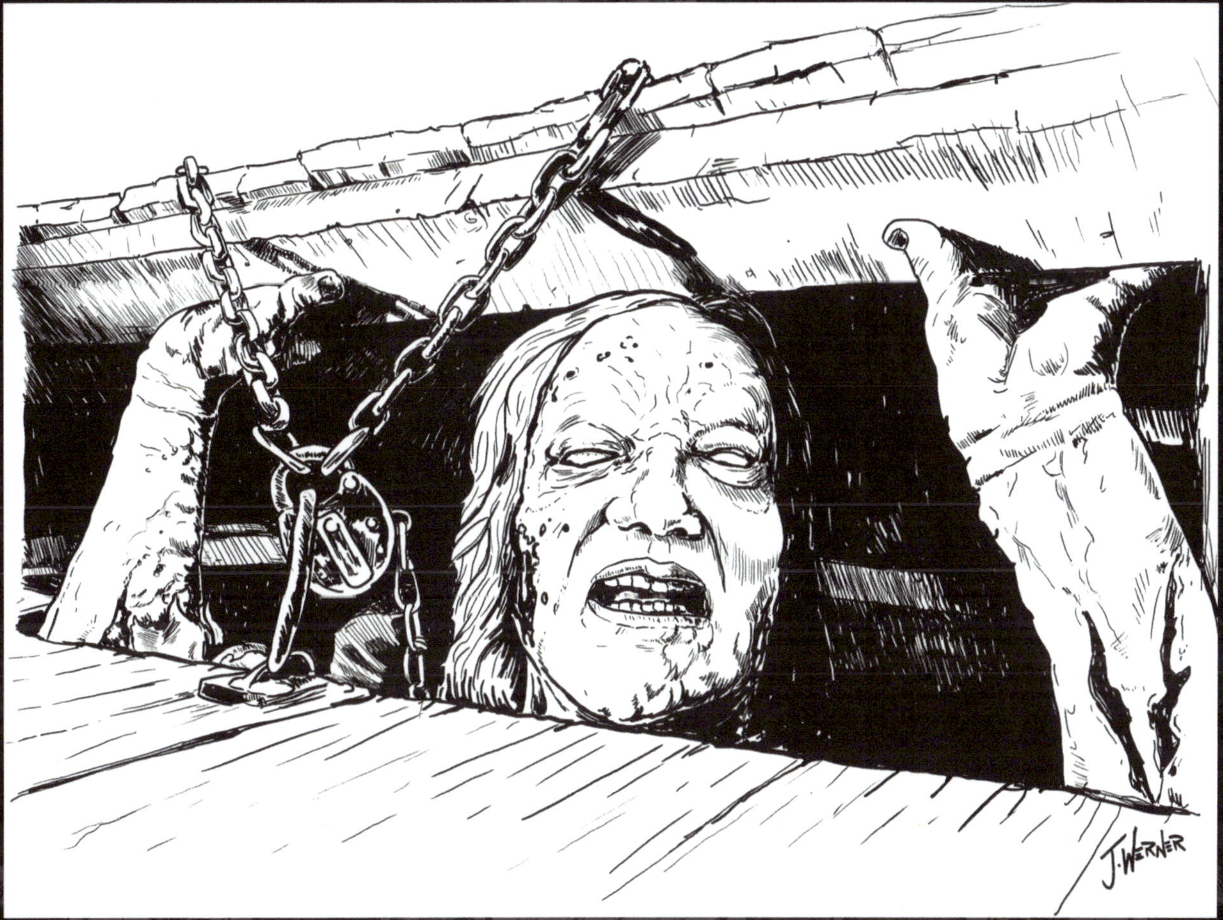

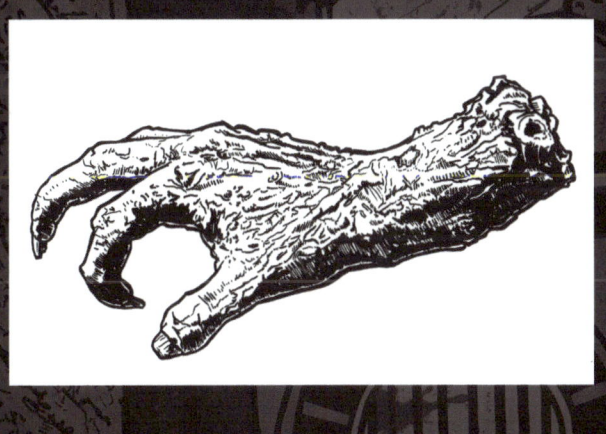
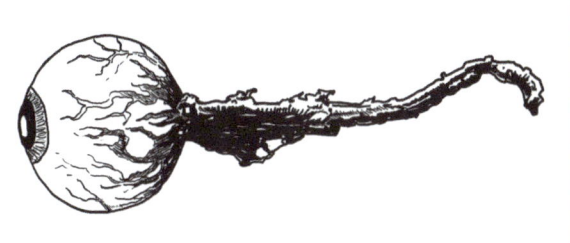
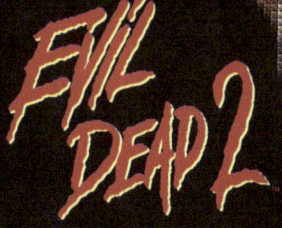

Some of my illustrations that appeared in the book *Evil Dead 2: The Book of the Thread*. Published by Source Point Press.

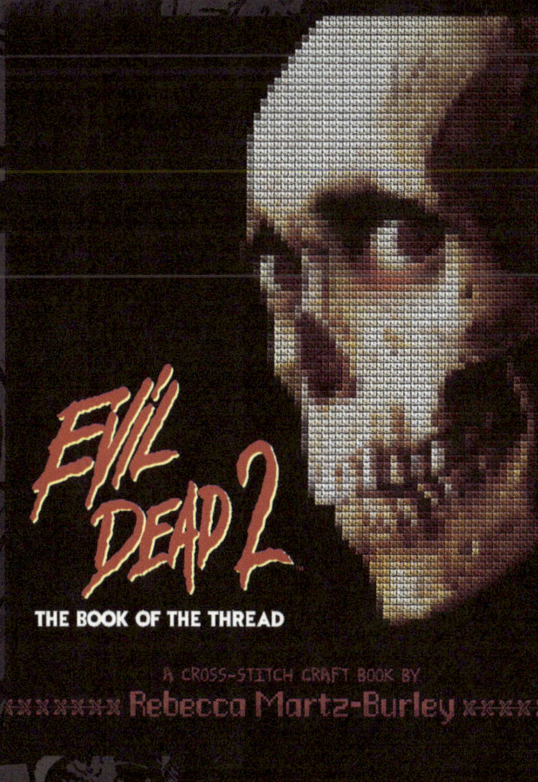

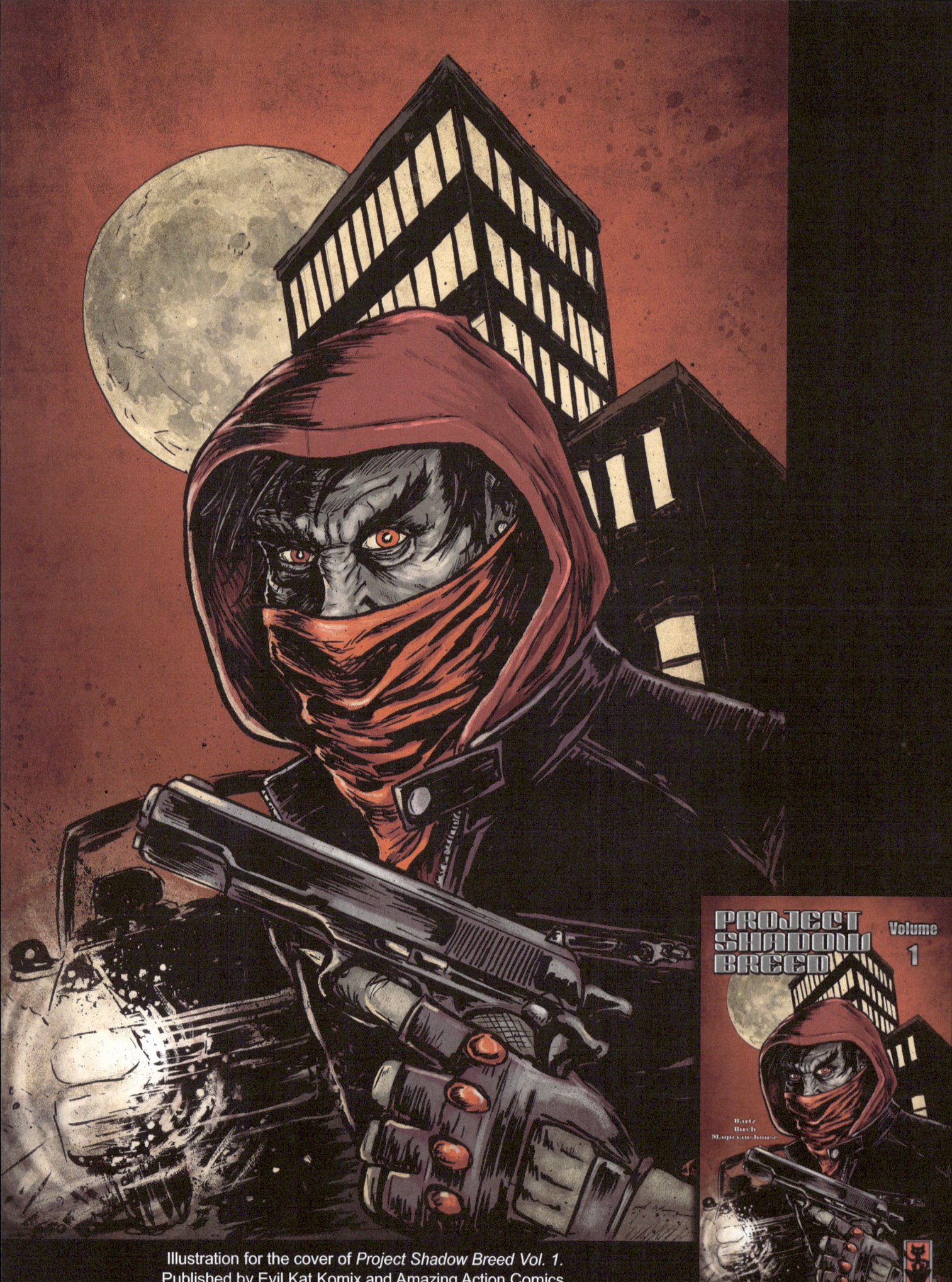

Illustration for the cover of *Project Shadow Breed Vol. 1*.
Published by Evil Kat Komix and Amazing Action Comics.

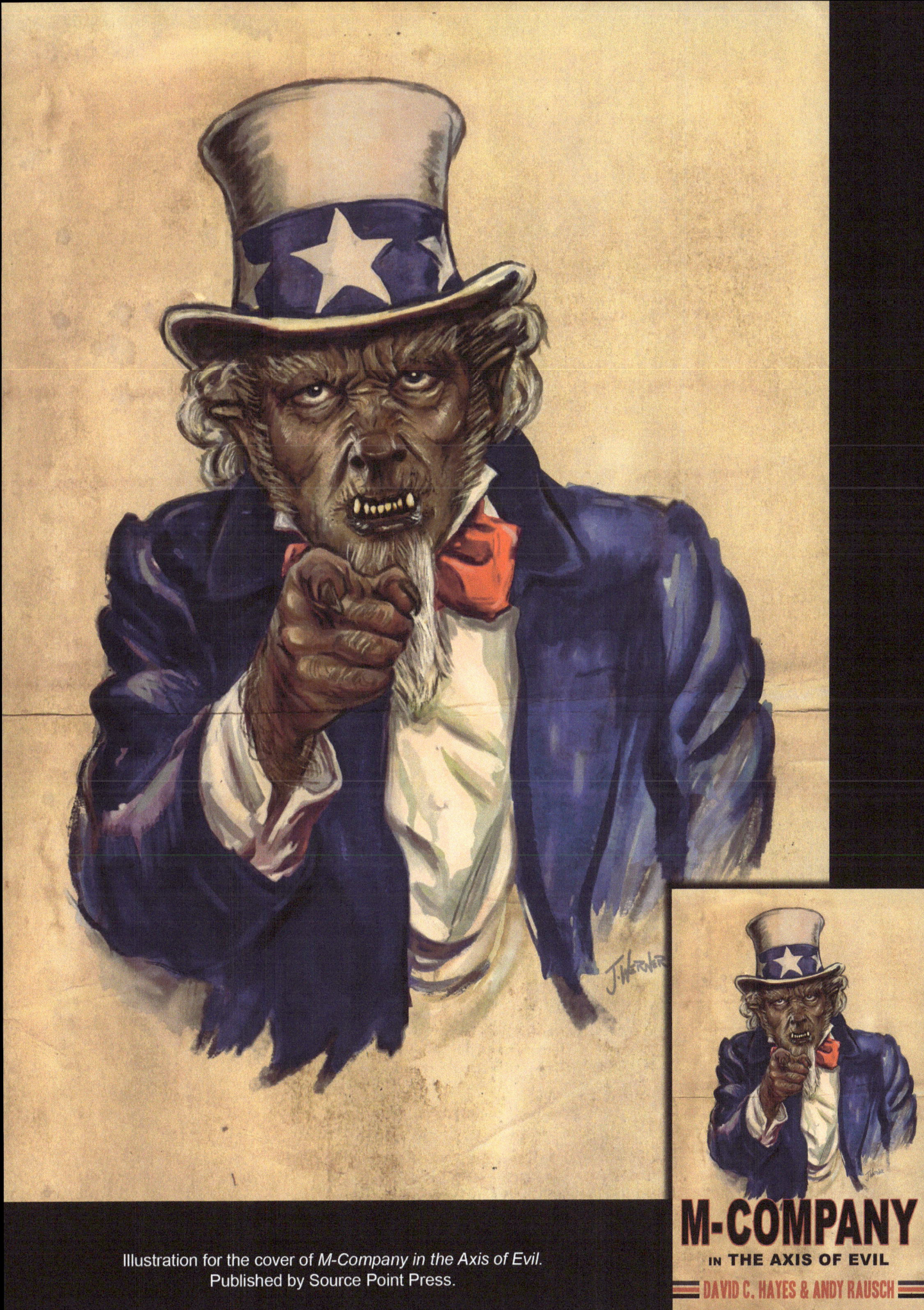

Illustration for the cover of *M-Company in the Axis of Evil*. Published by Source Point Press.

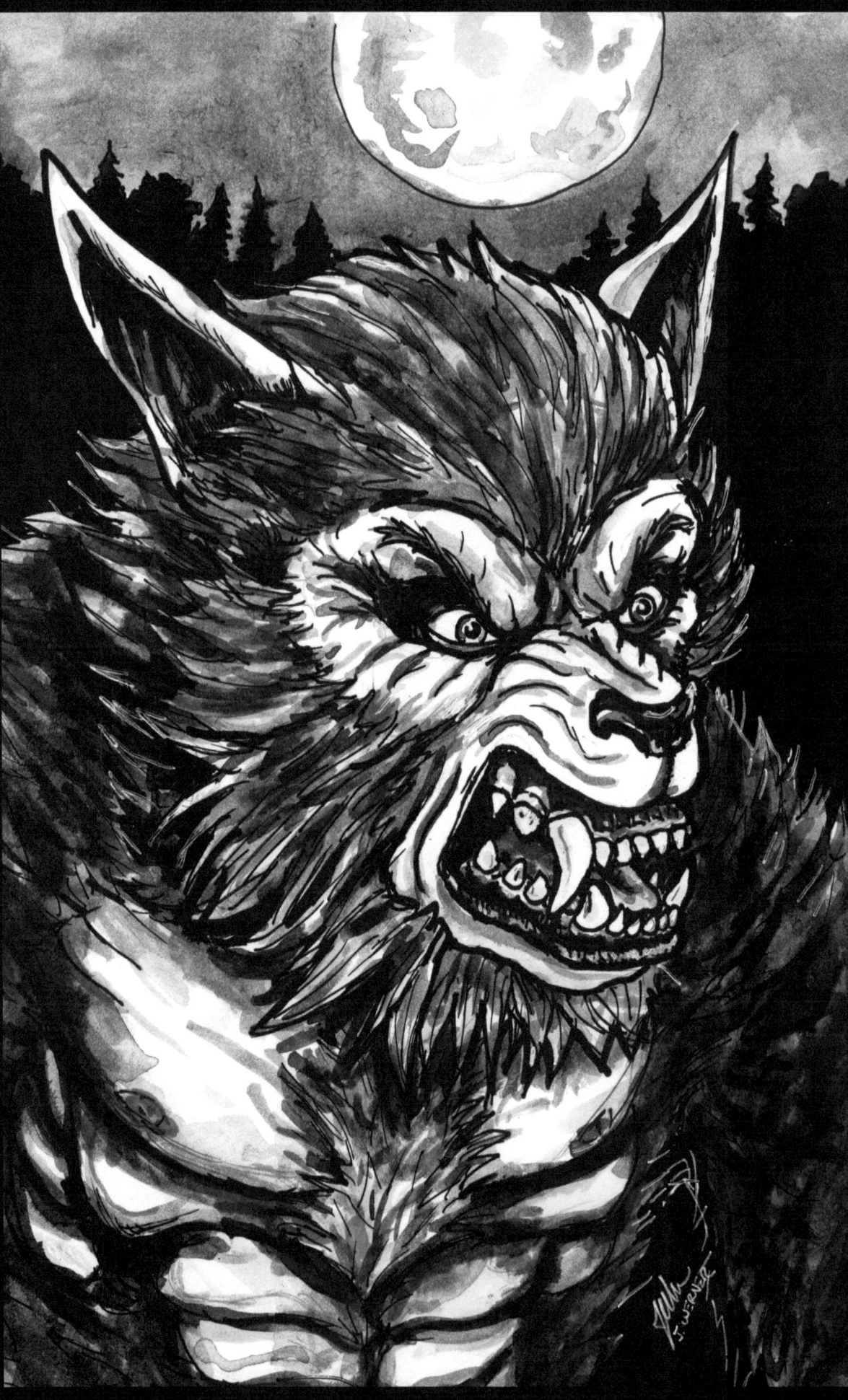

Ink illustration that appeared in the book Lycan Lore published by Source Point Press.

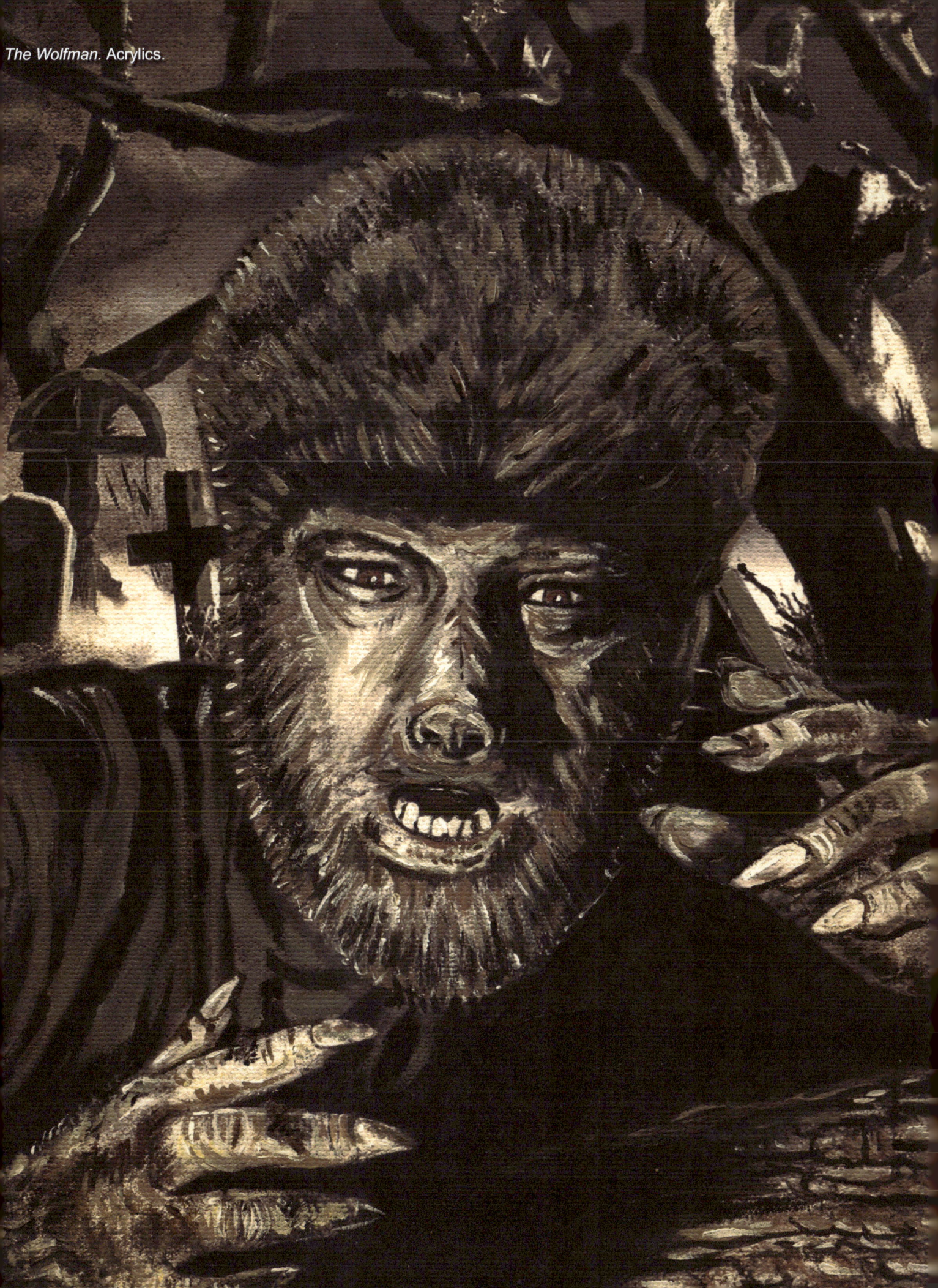
The Wolfman. Acrylics.

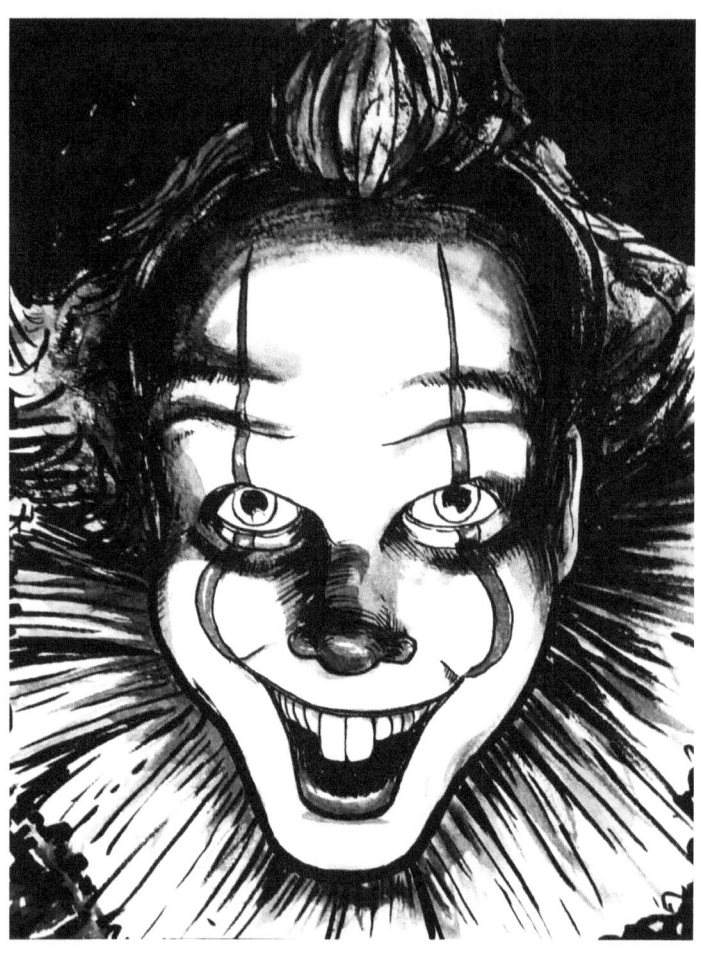
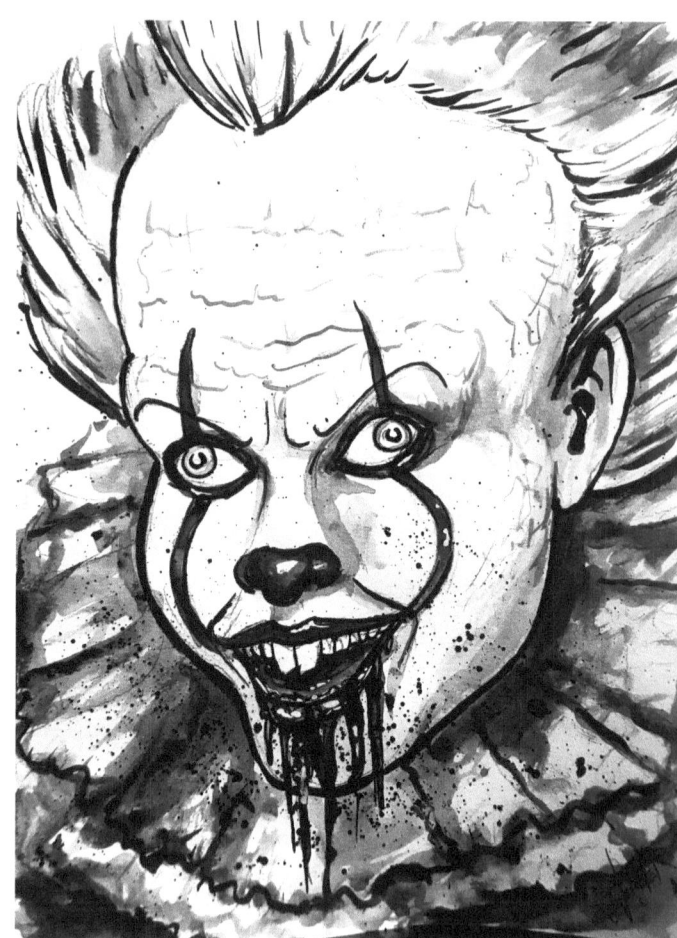

Various sketches done at conventions.

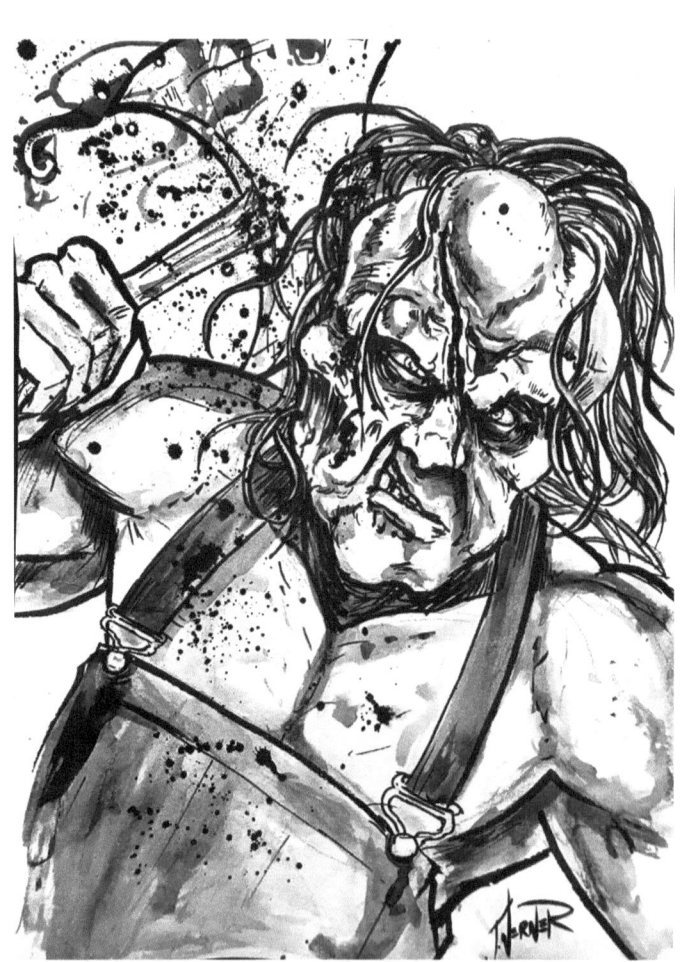
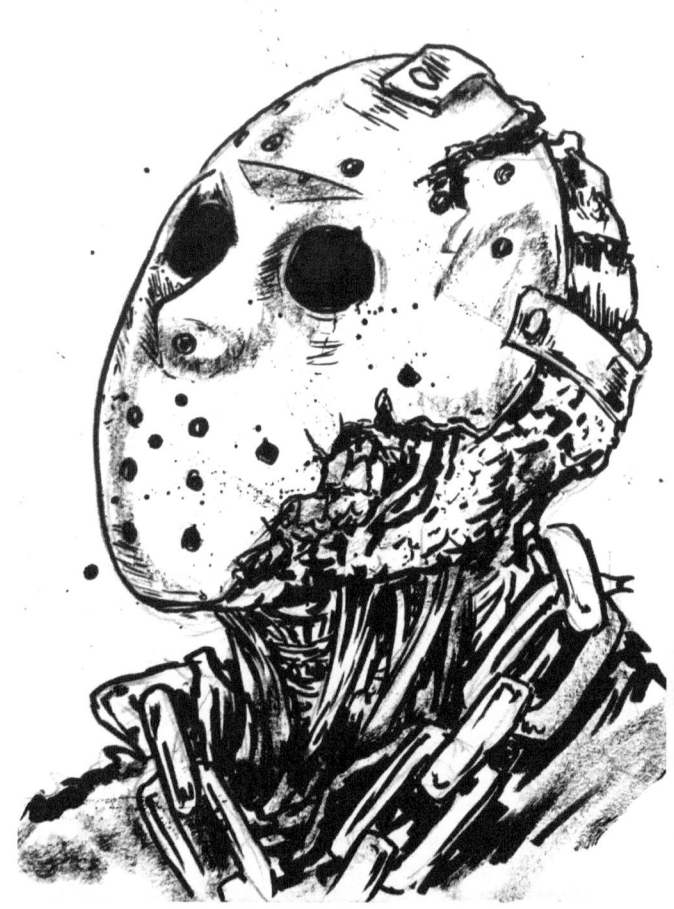

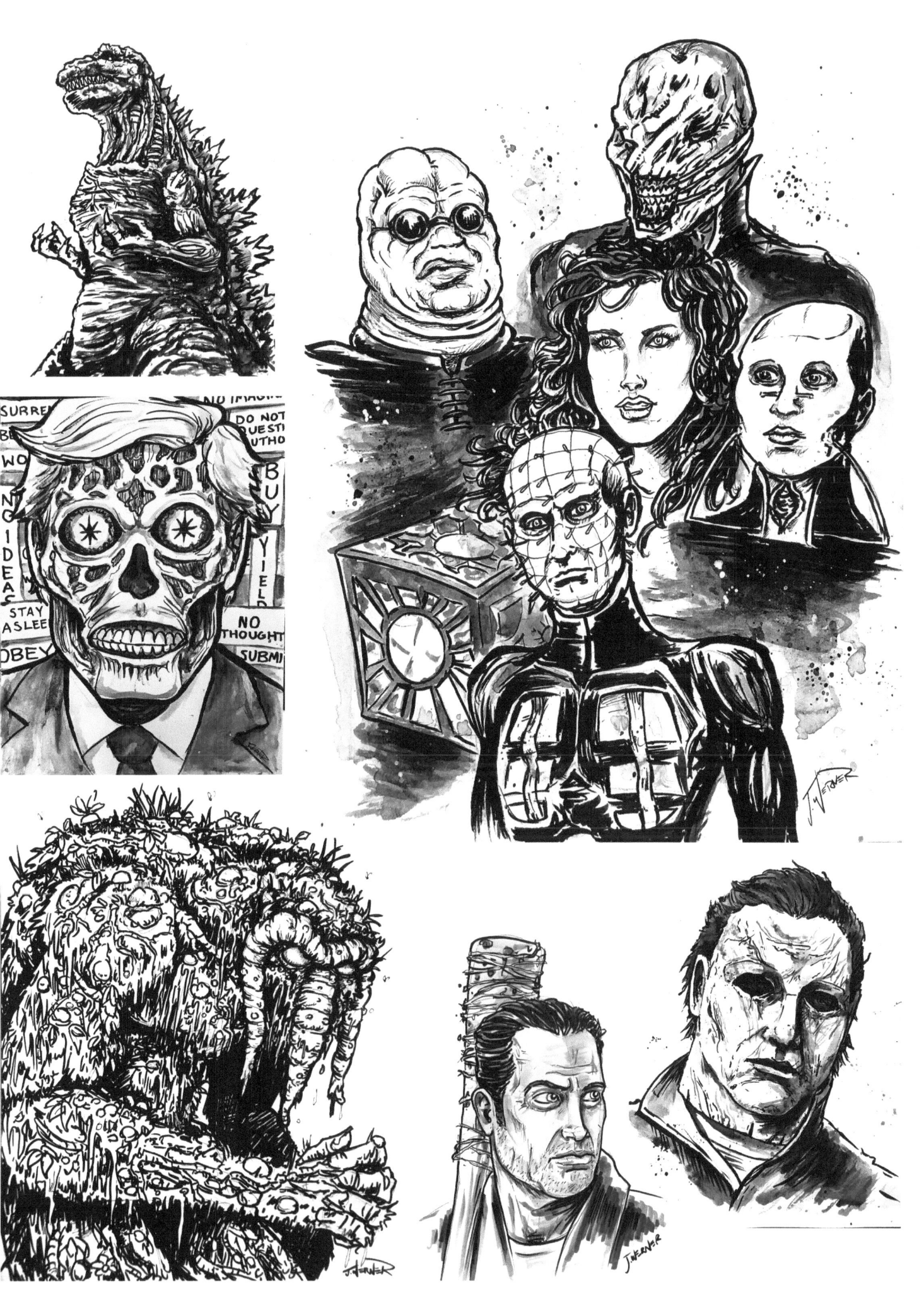

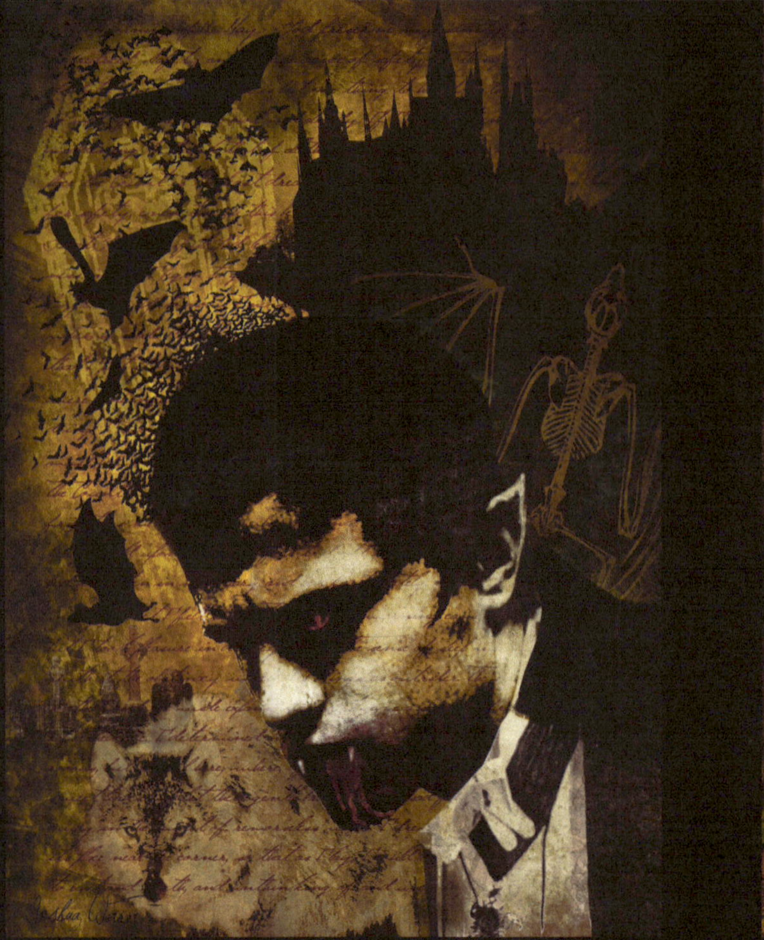

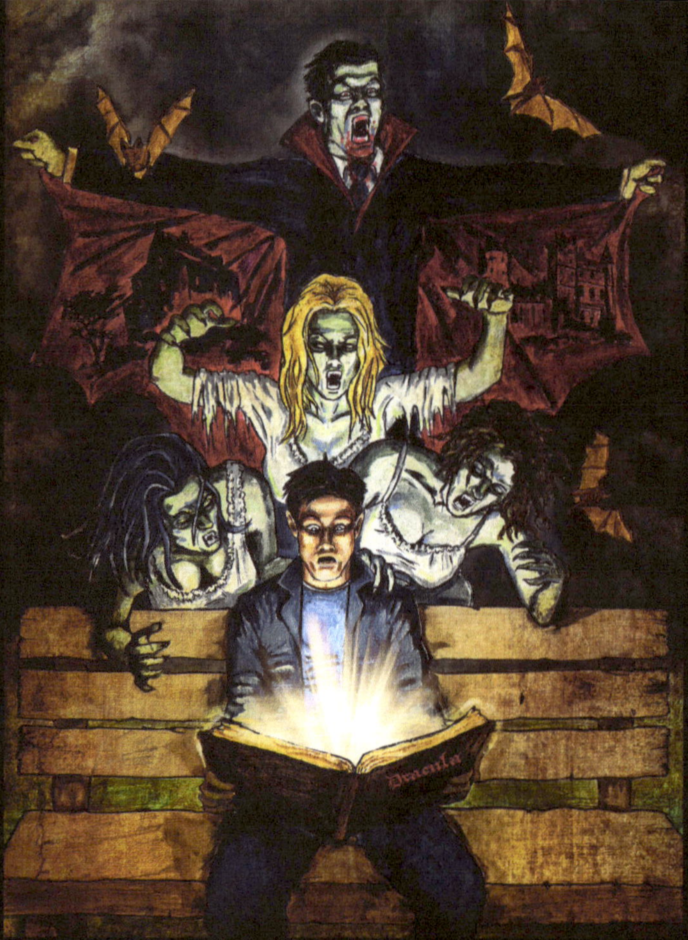

Base card set illustrations and a few of the sketchcards I did for the *Dracula* trading card set published by Cult-Stuff.

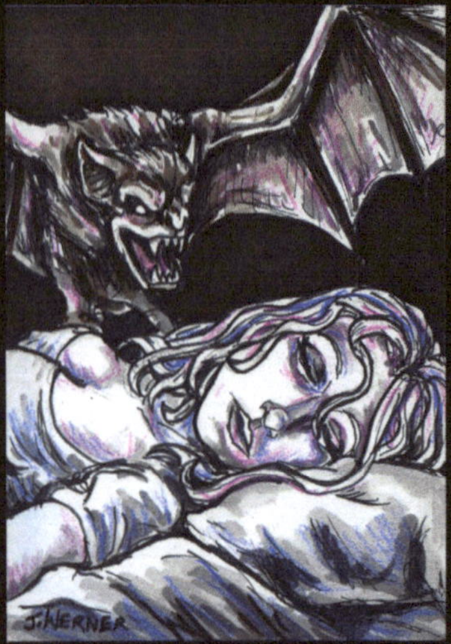

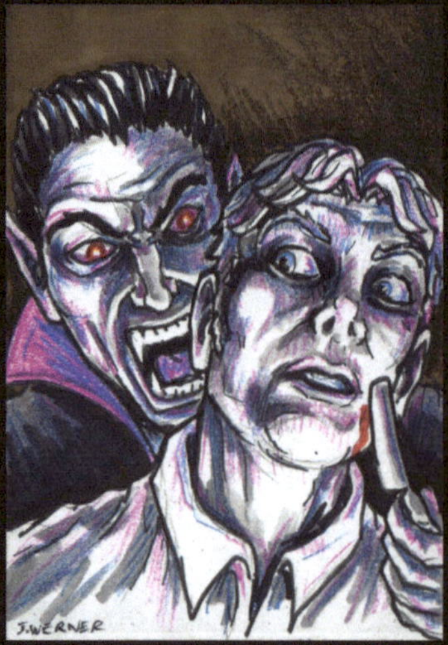

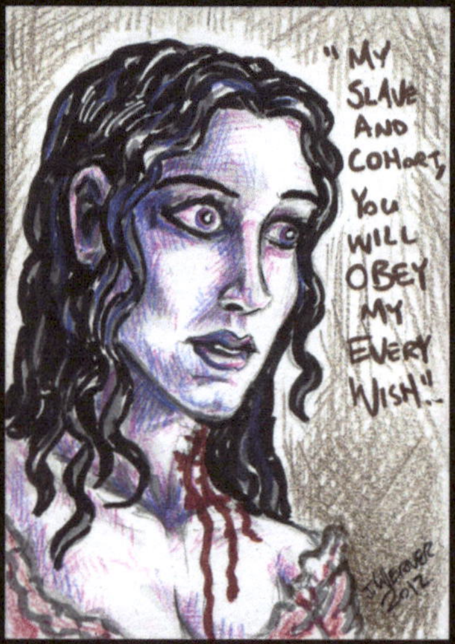

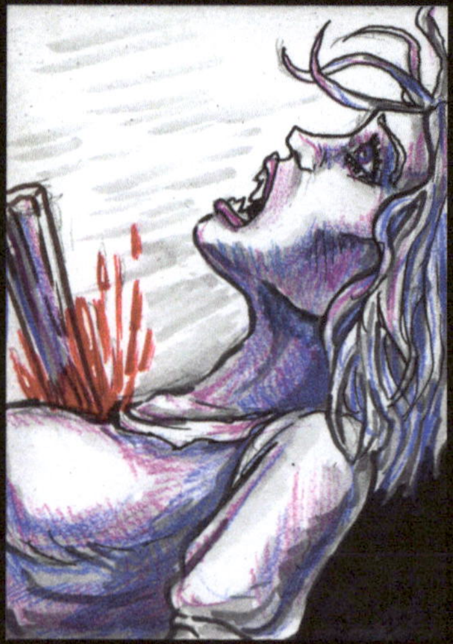

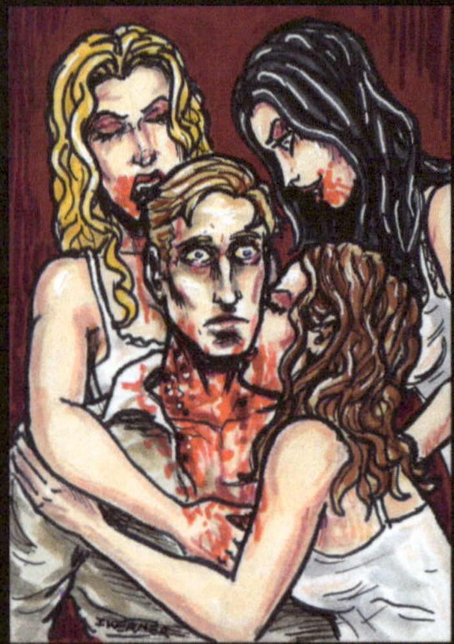

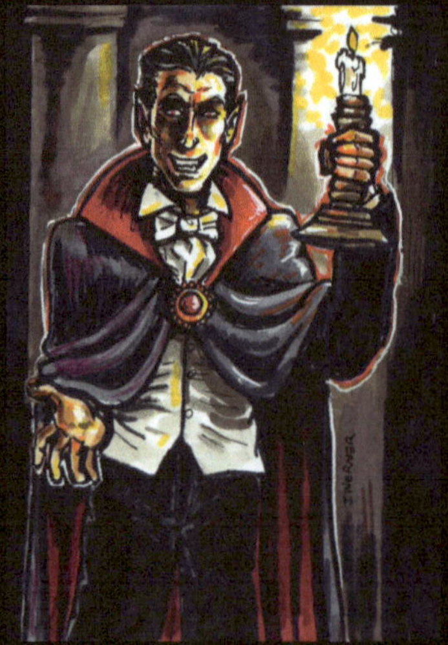

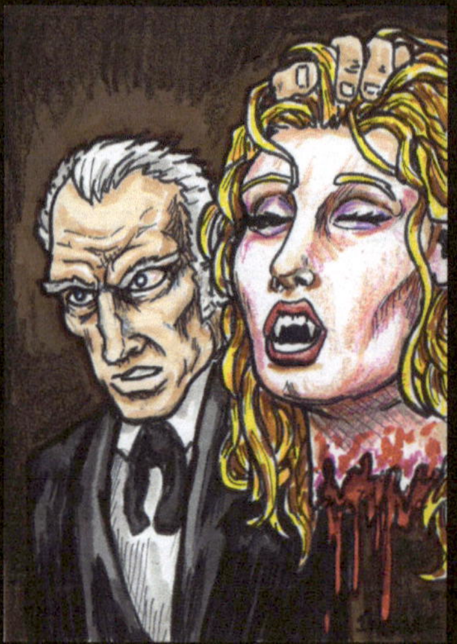

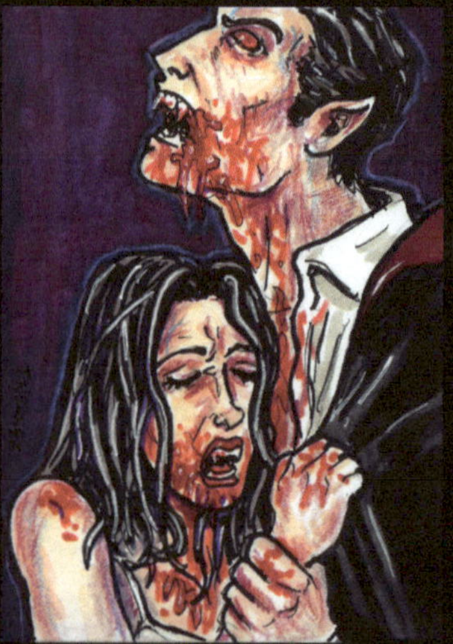

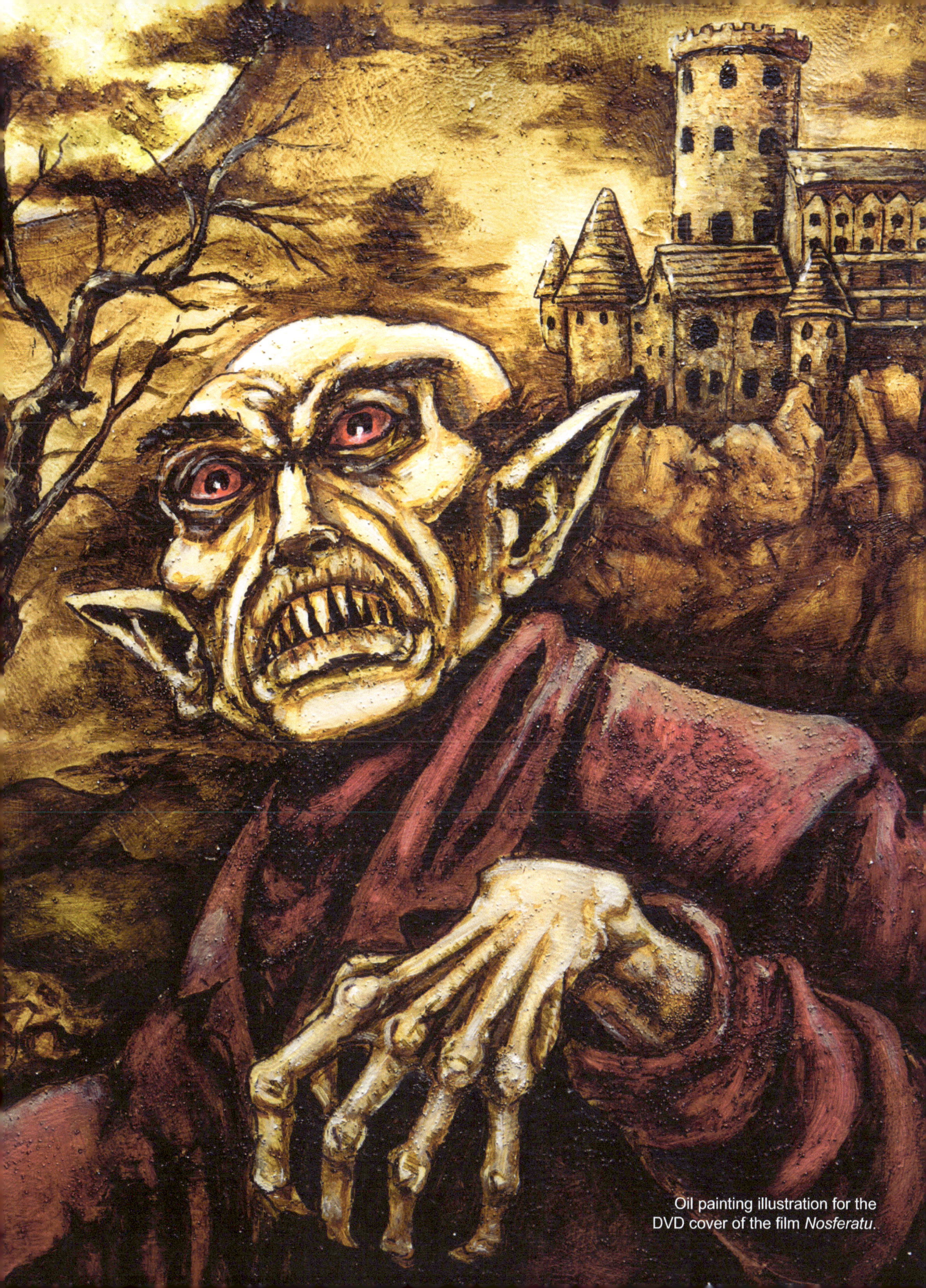
Oil painting illustration for the DVD cover of the film *Nosferatu*.

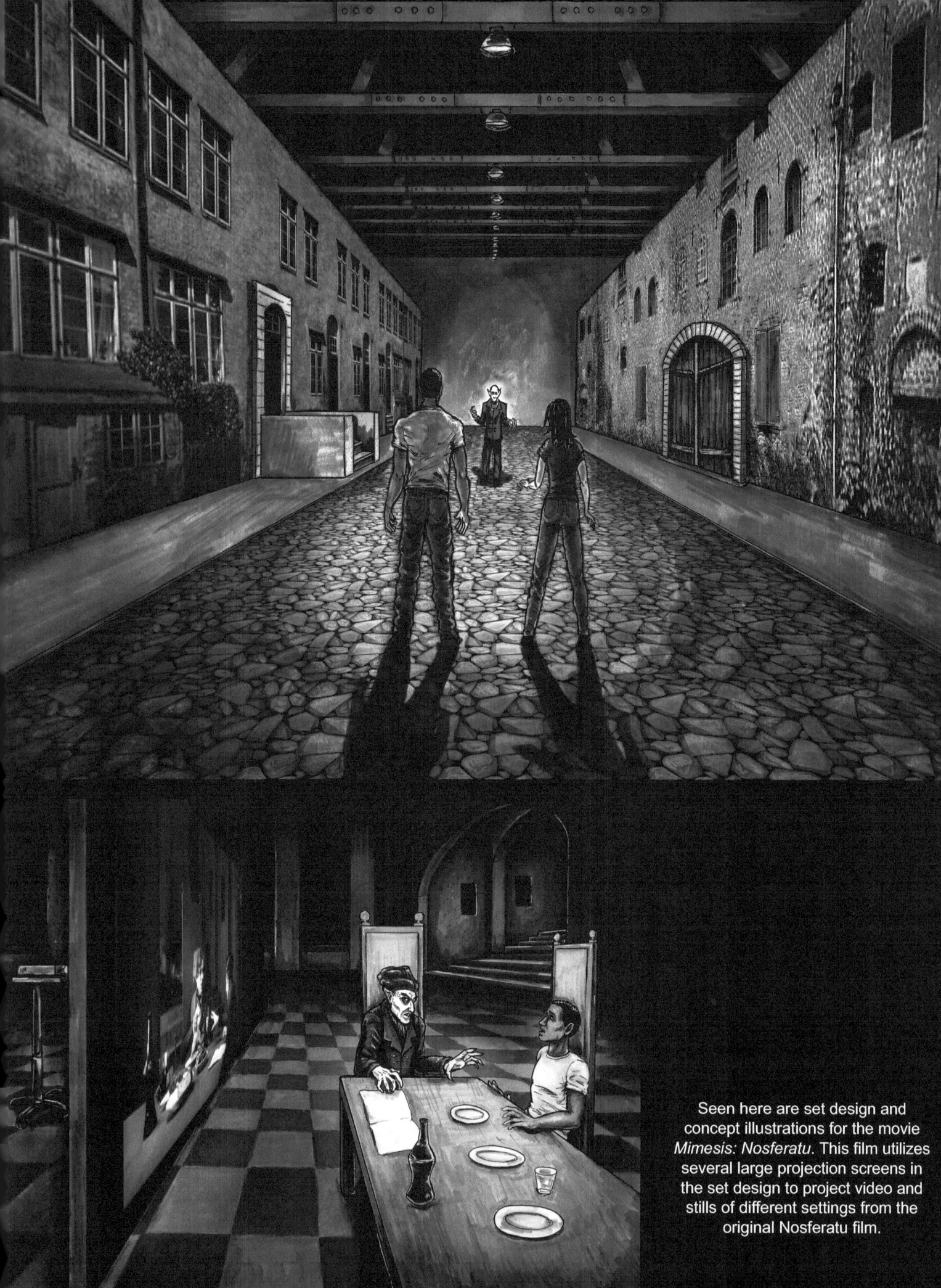

Seen here are set design and concept illustrations for the movie *Mimesis: Nosferatu*. This film utilizes several large projection screens in the set design to project video and stills of different settings from the original Nosferatu film.

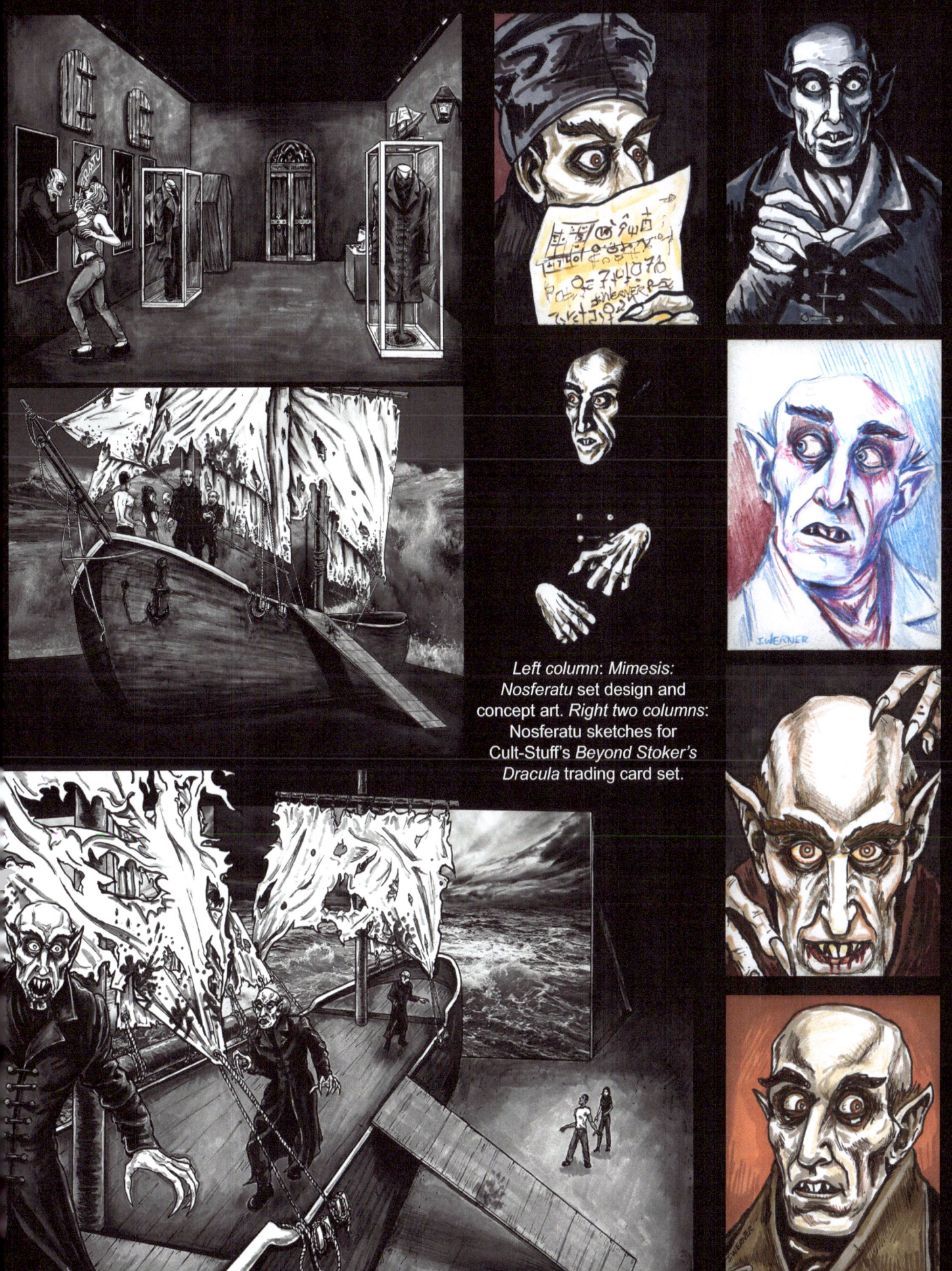

Left column: *Mimesis: Nosferatu* set design and concept art. Right two columns: Nosferatu sketches for Cult-Stuff's *Beyond Stoker's Dracula* trading card set.

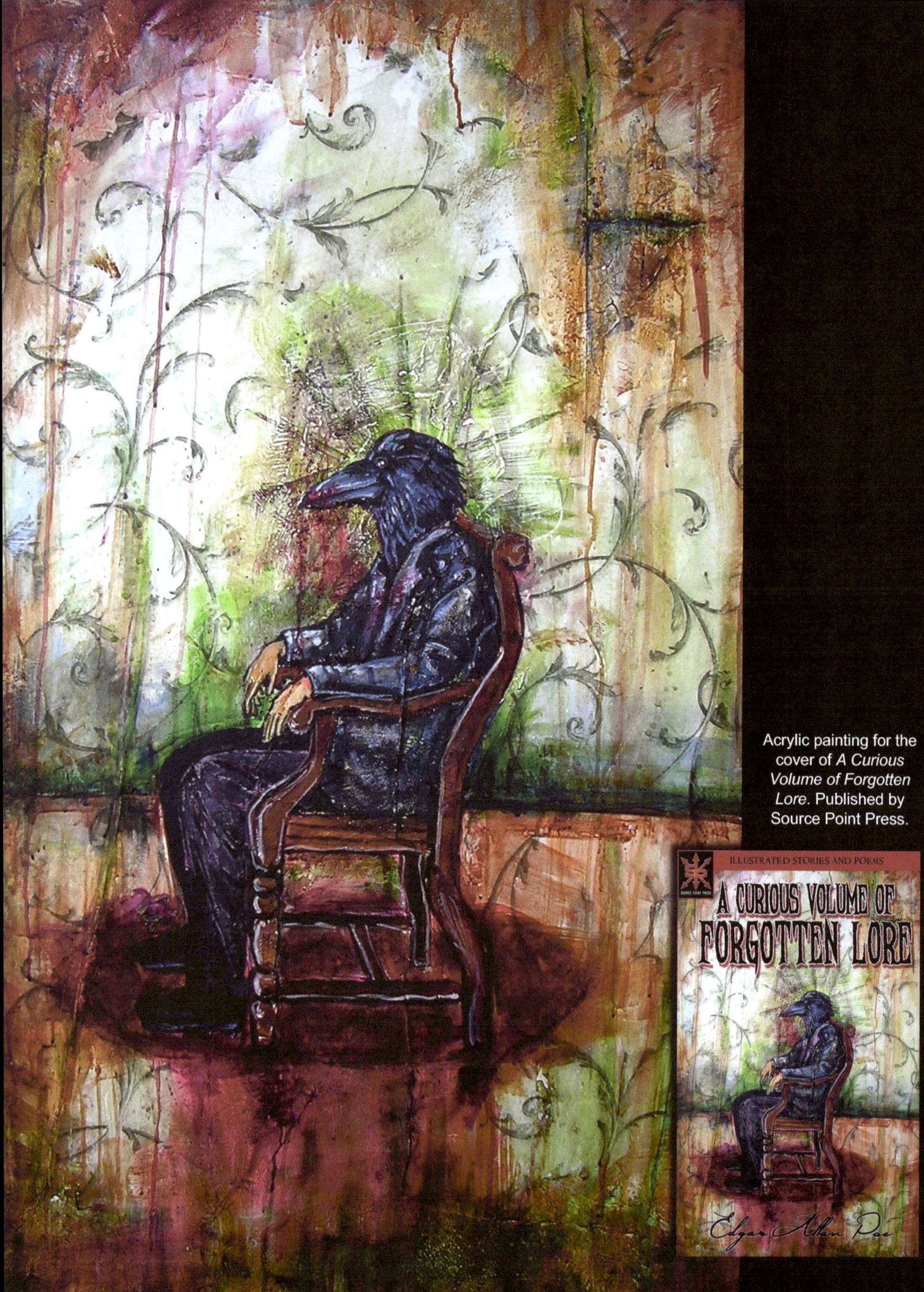

Acrylic painting for the cover of *A Curious Volume of Forgotten Lore*. Published by Source Point Press.

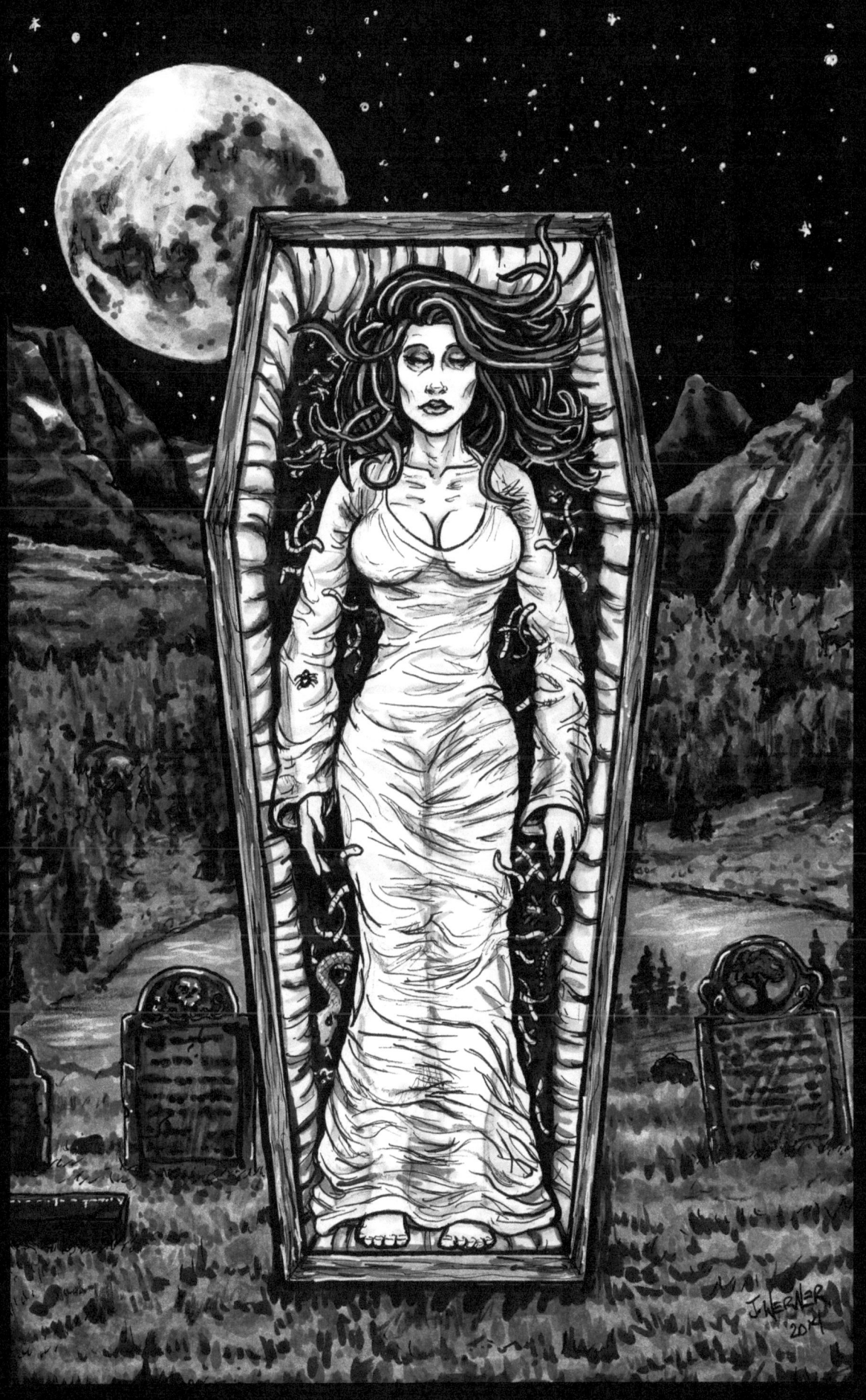

Illustration for the poem "The Sleeper" by Edgar Allan Poe.
Published in the book *A Curious Volume of Forgotten Lore* by Source Point Press.

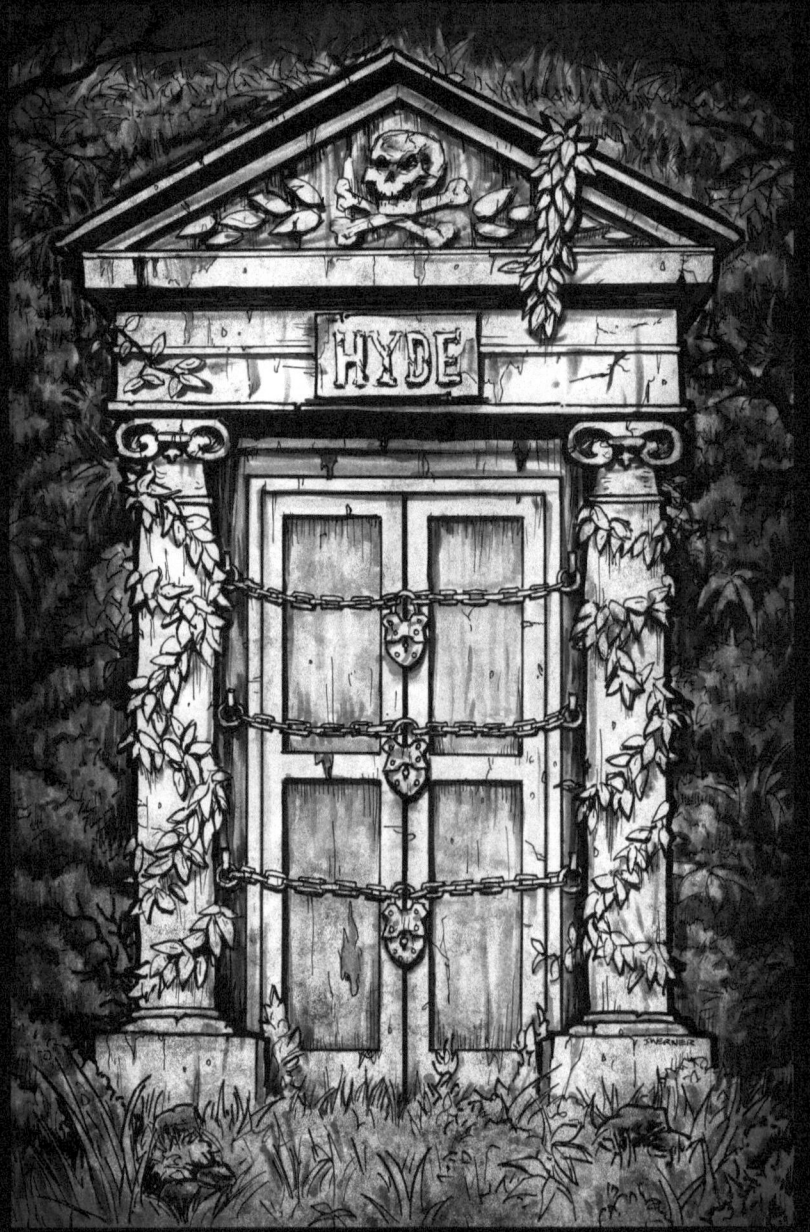
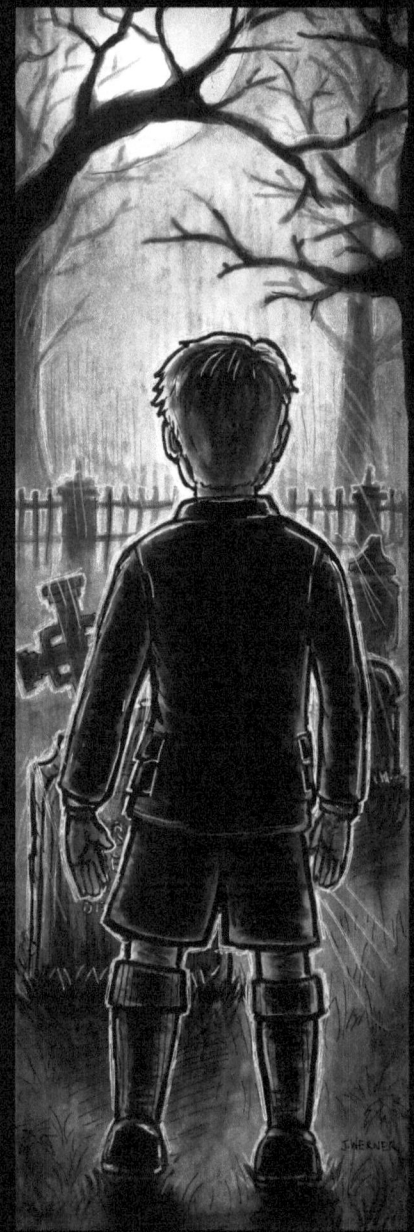
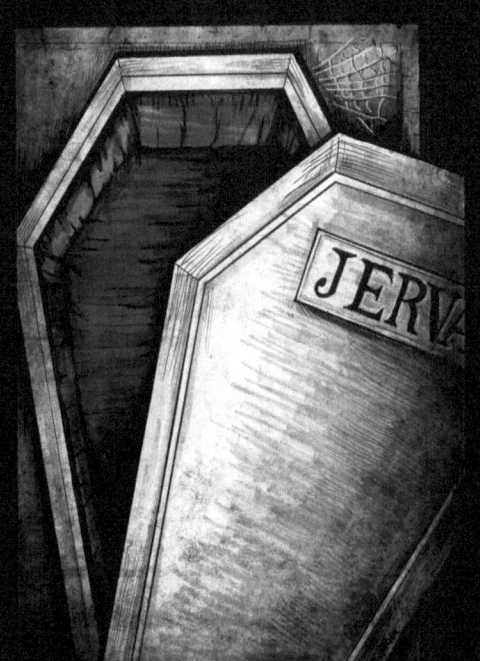
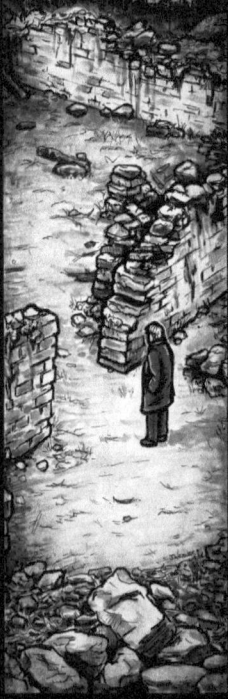

Illustrations for the story "The Tomb" by H.P. Lovecraft.

Published in *H.P. Lovecraft: The Tomb* and *H.P. Lovecraft: The Early Stories* by Caliber Comics.

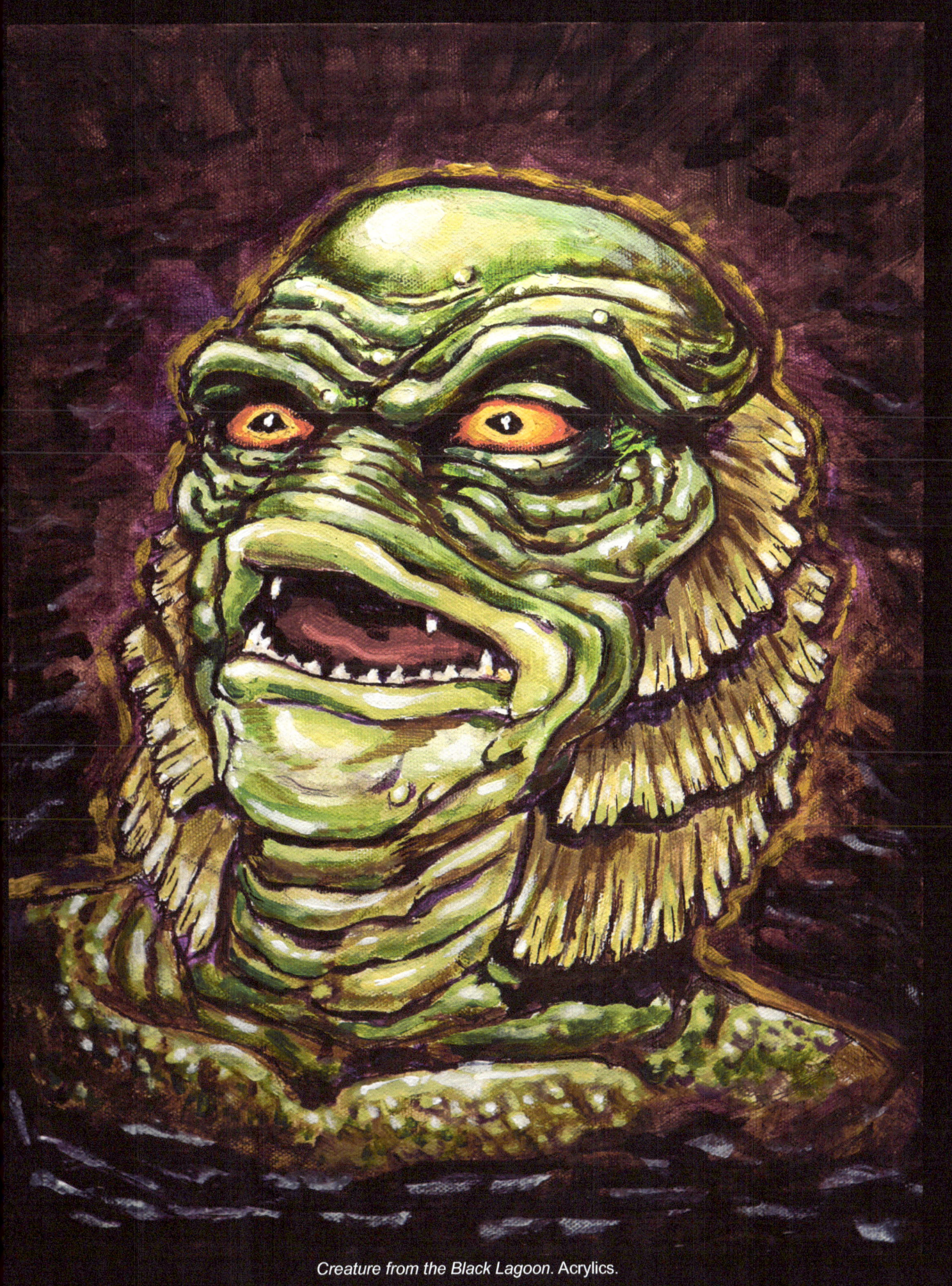

Creature from the Black Lagoon. Acrylics.

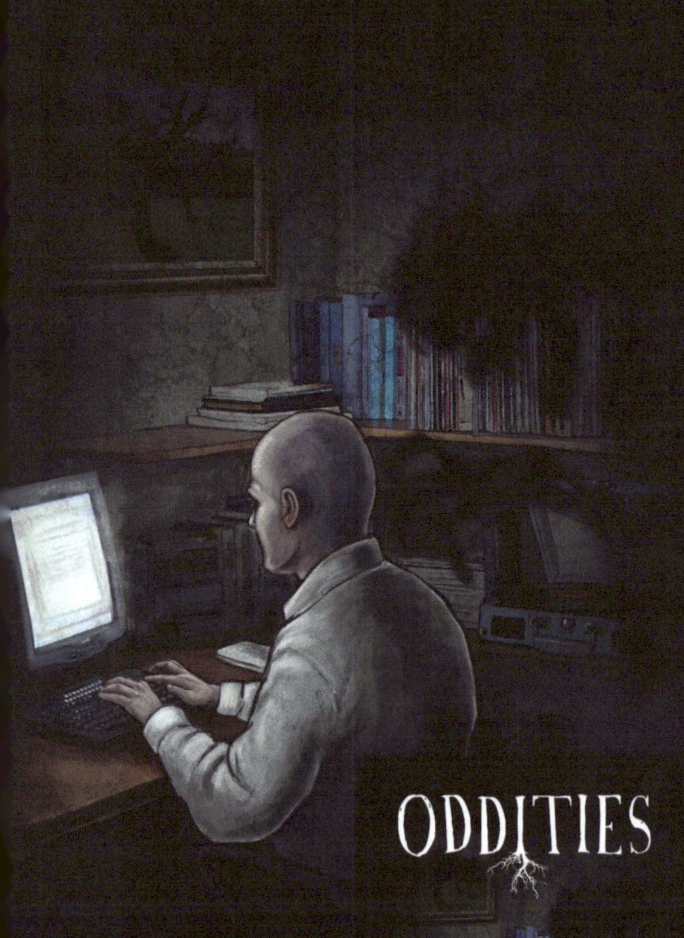

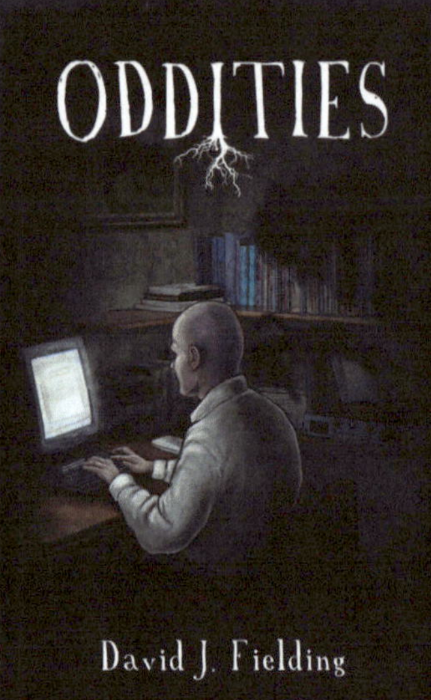

ODDITIES

David J. Fielding

Illustration for the cover of *Oddities*. Published by Source Point Press.

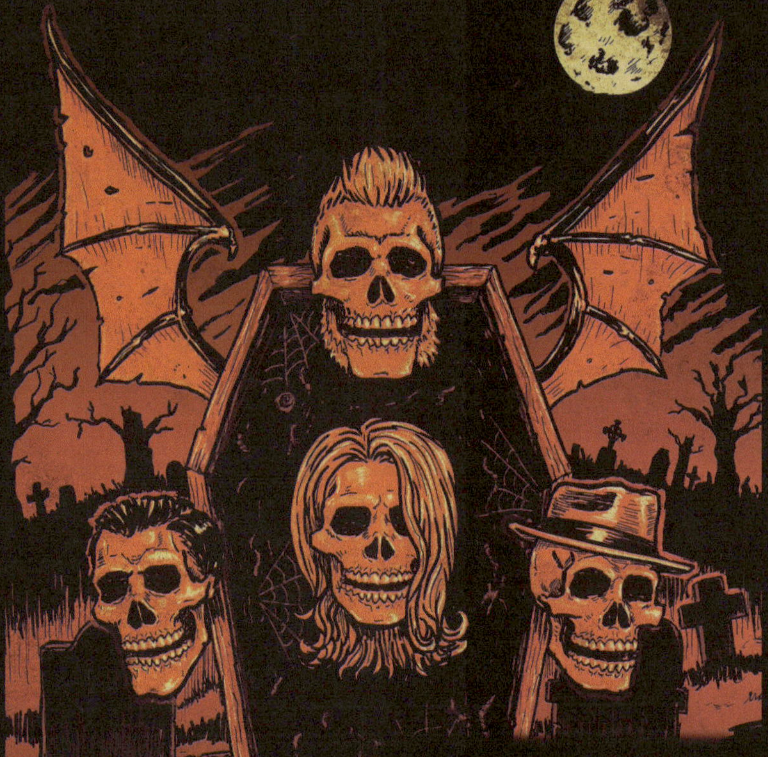

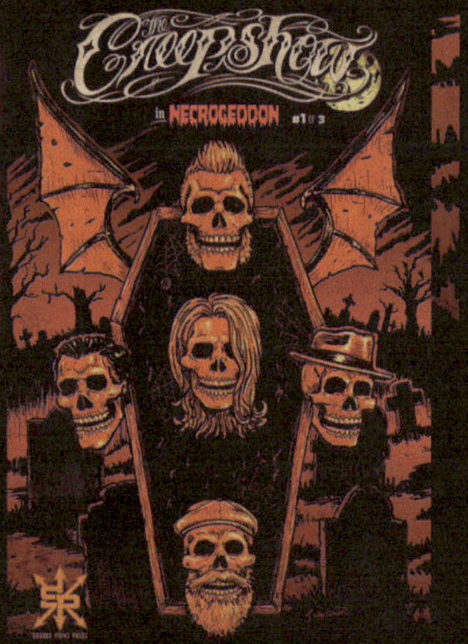

Illustration for the cover of *The Creepshow in Necrogeddon #1*. Published by Source Point Press.

Shown here are a few of the sketches I did for *The Wickerman* trading card set from Unstoppable Cards.

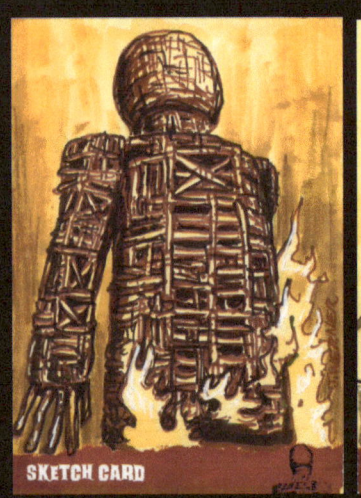
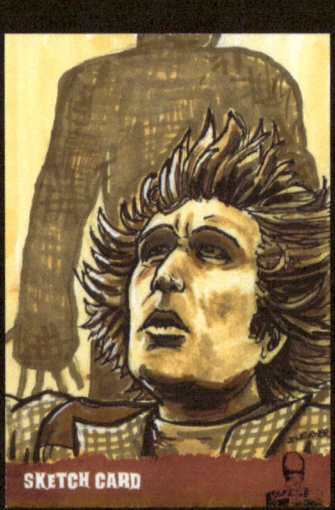
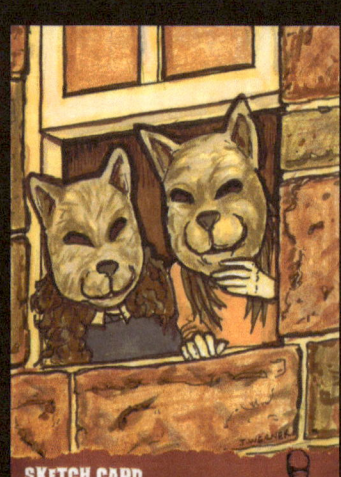
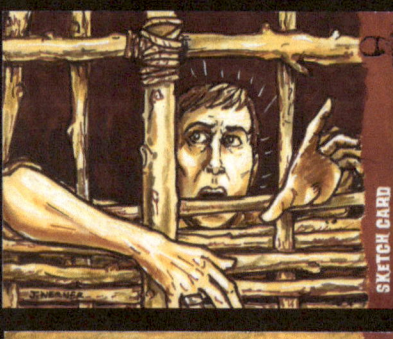
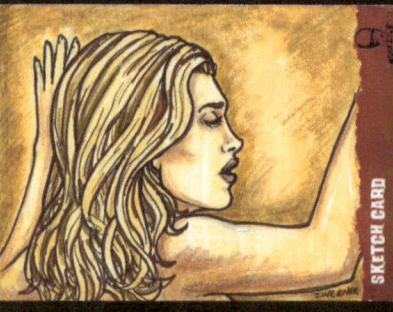

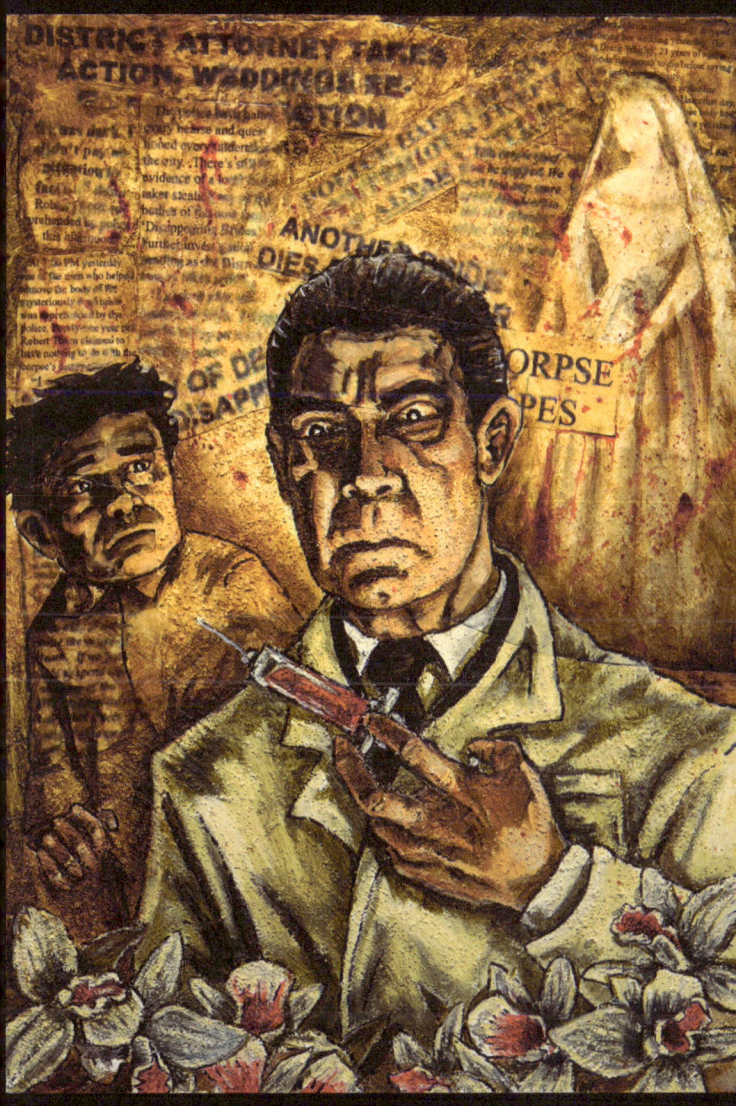
Oil painting illustration for the DVD cover of the film *The Corpse Vanishes*.

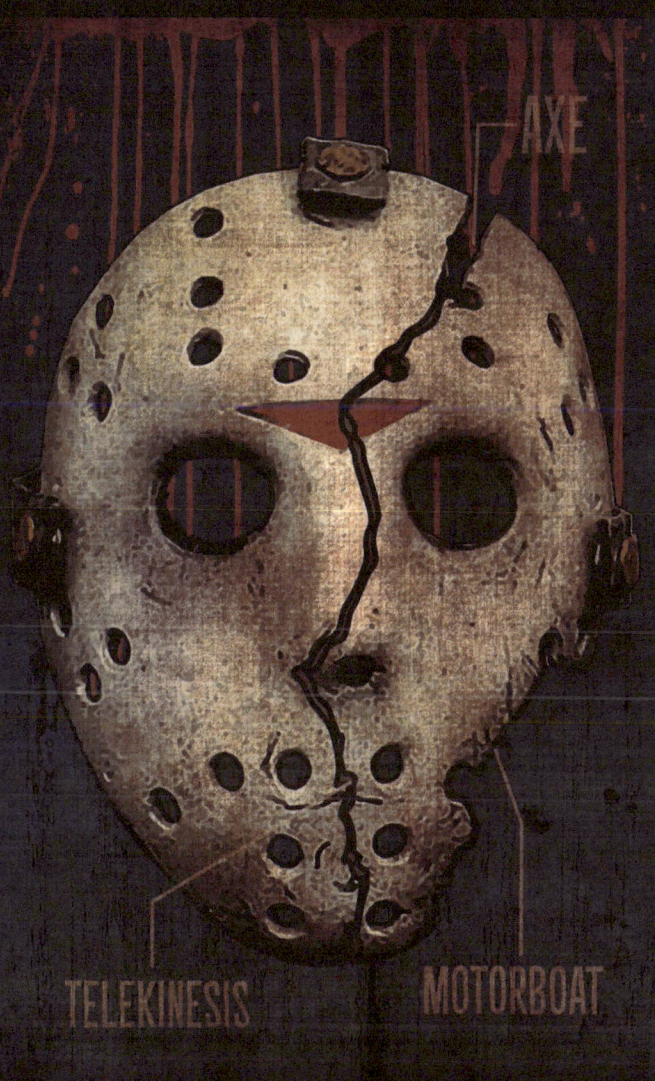
Mask Wounds. Mixed media.

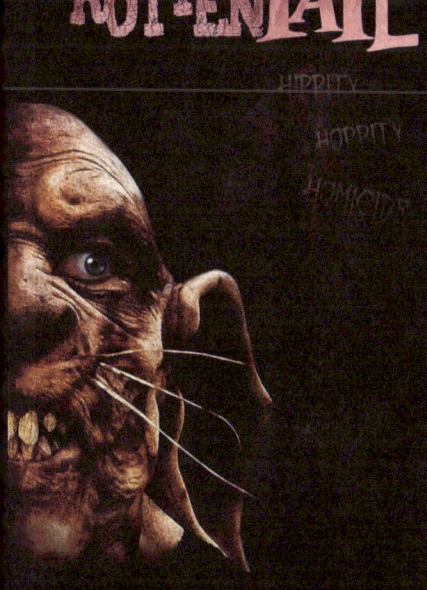
Poster and Blu-ray Cover artwork for the movie *Rottentail*.

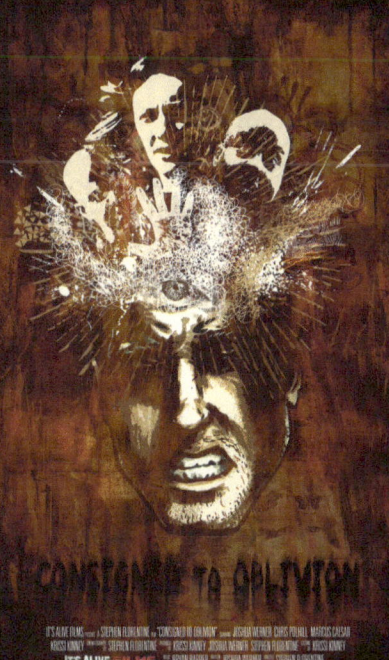
Poster artwork for the movie *Consigned to Oblivion*.

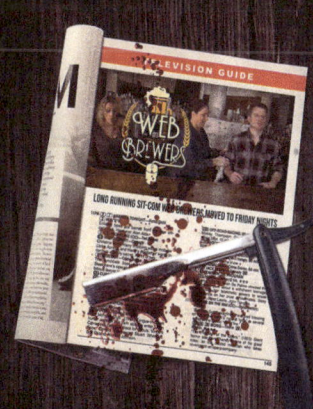
Poster artwork for the movie *Friday Night Death Slot*.

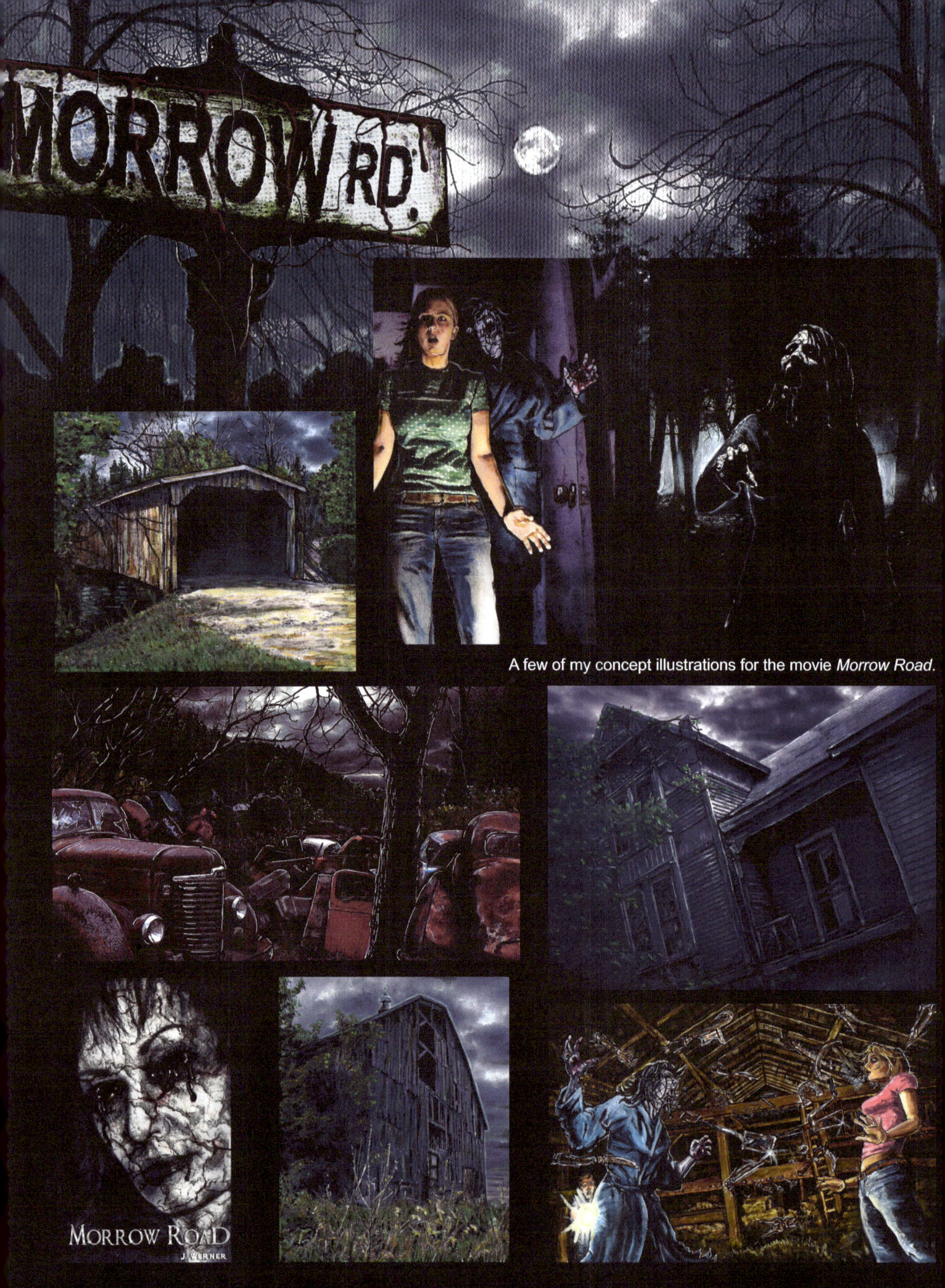

A few of my concept illustrations for the movie *Morrow Road*.

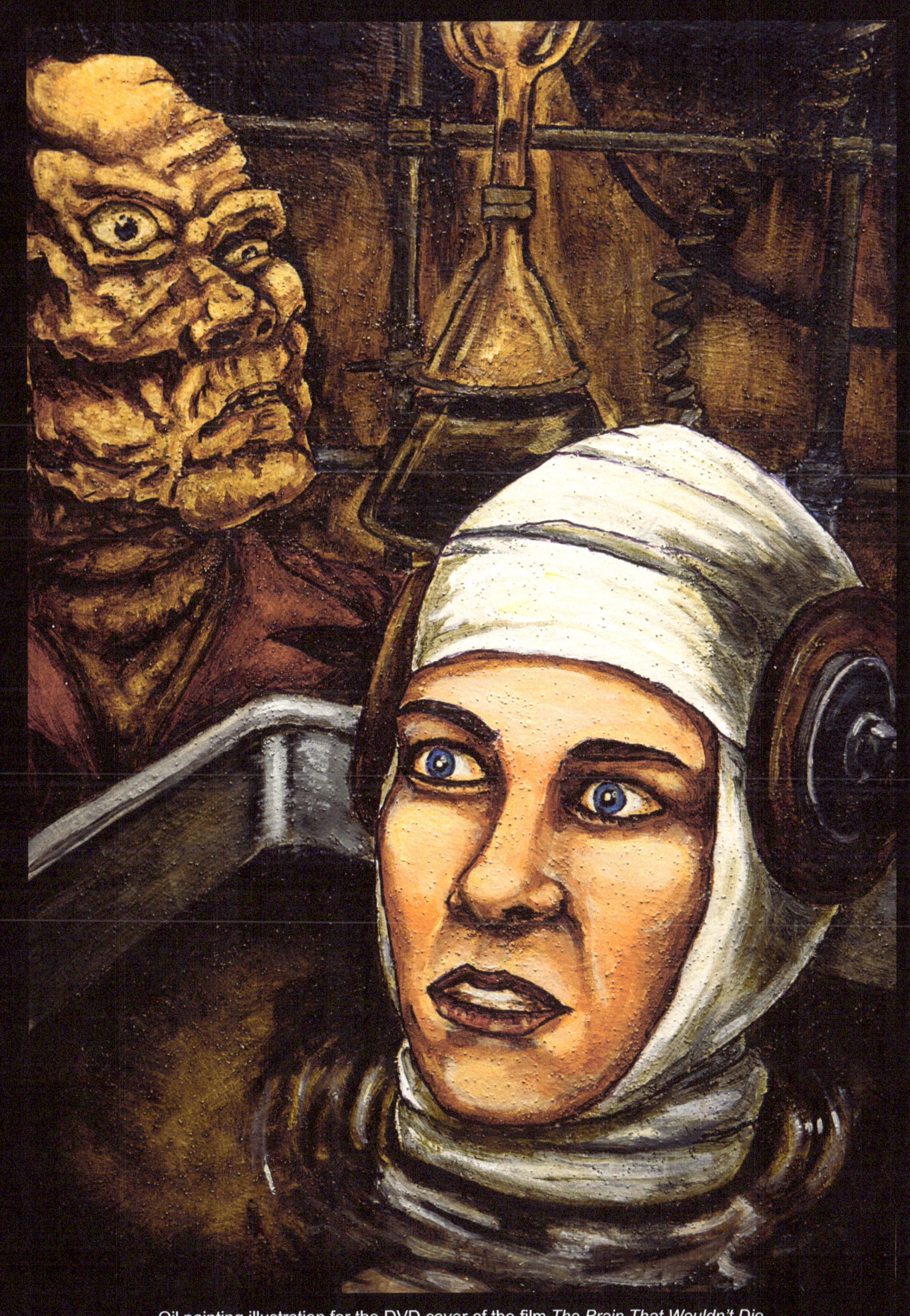
Oil painting illustration for the DVD cover of the film *The Brain That Wouldn't Die*.

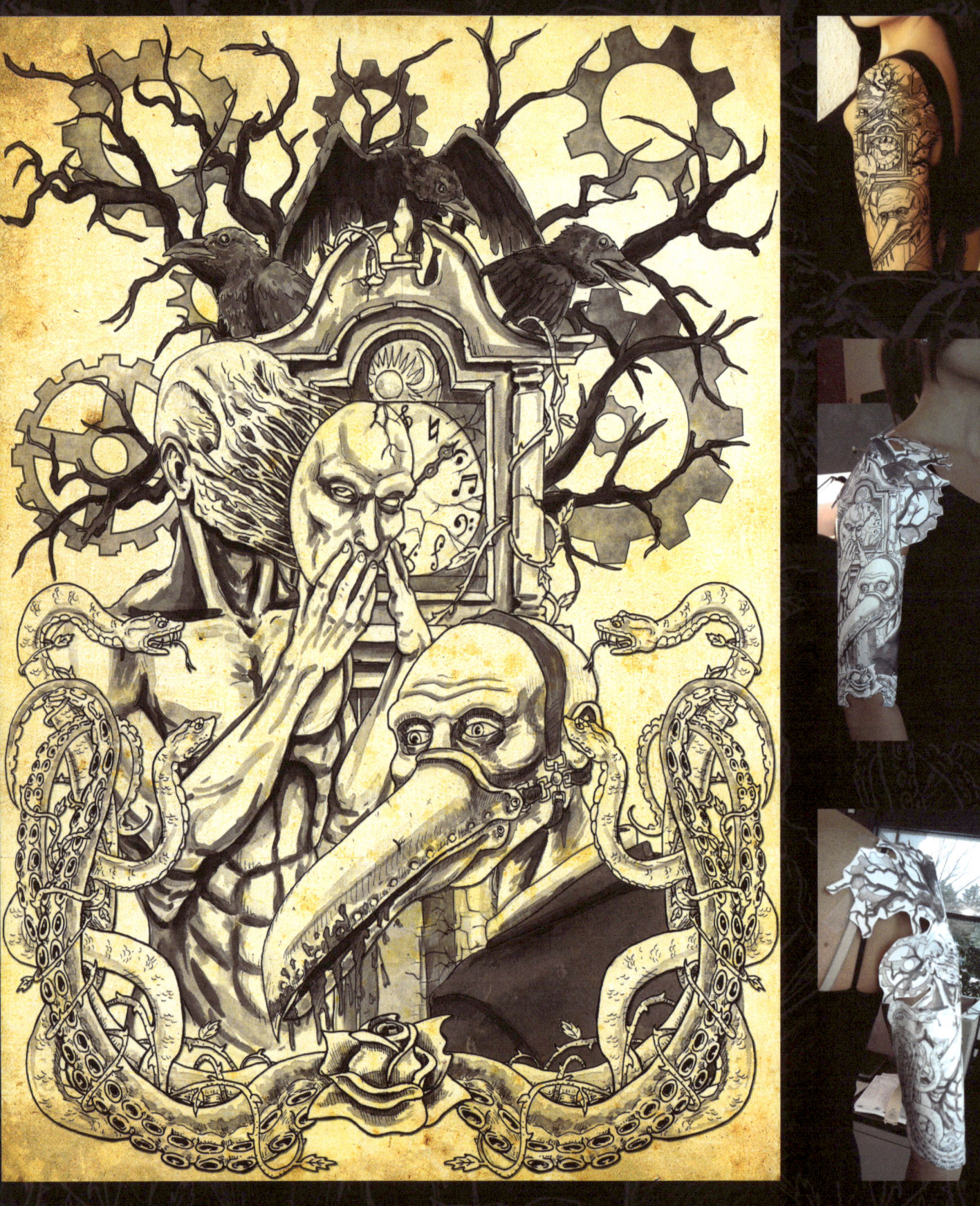

Above Left: Commissioned illustration for a commissioned tattoo sleeves design.
Above Right: Rough mock-ups I created during the design process to determine placement, size, and spatial relationships.

While the client liked the design, tattoo itself was never done.

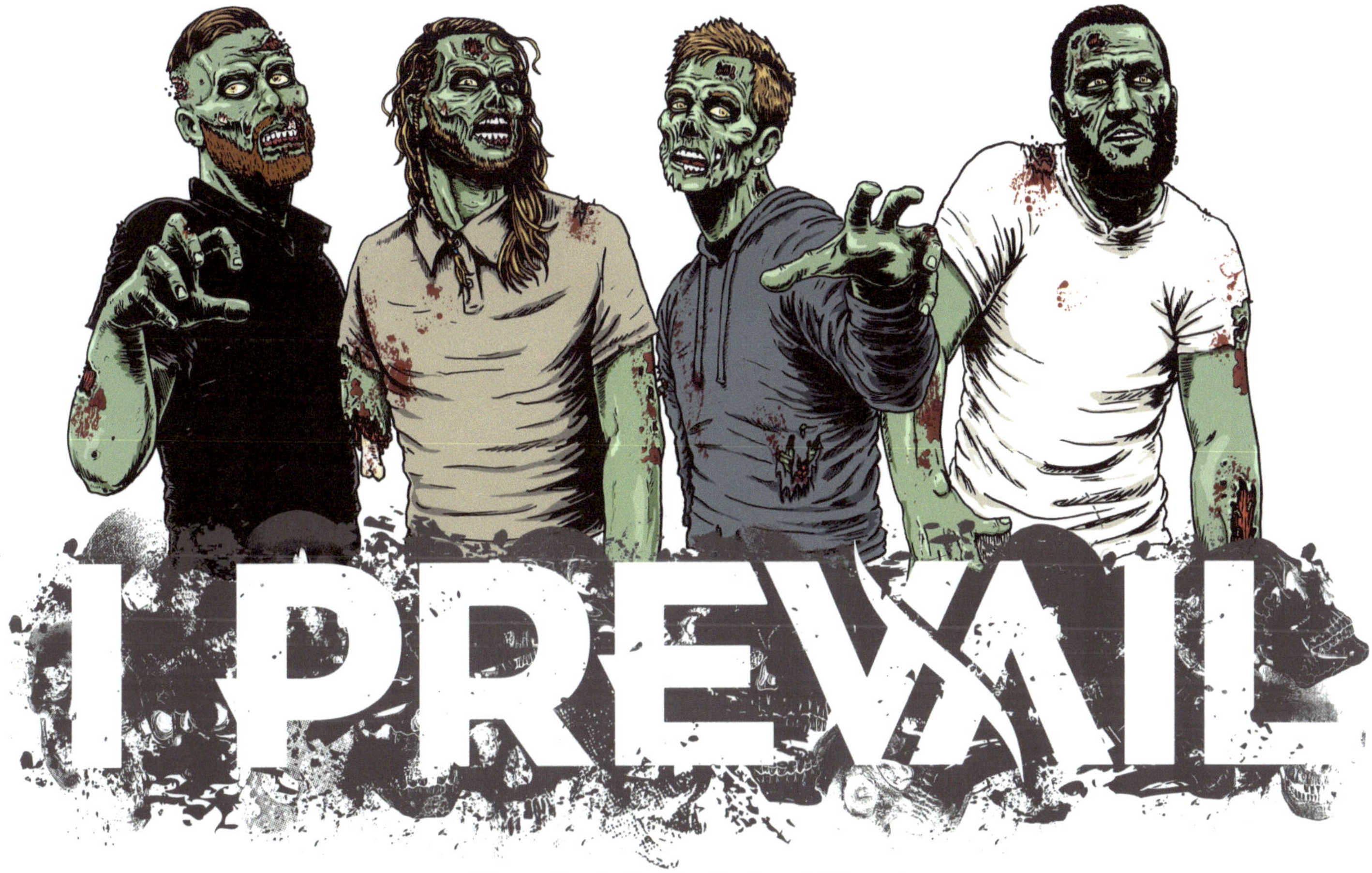

Above: Illustration for the band *I Prevail*.
Bottom left: Death and the Devil in the Old West. Ink. *Bottom right*: Werewolf mid-transformation.

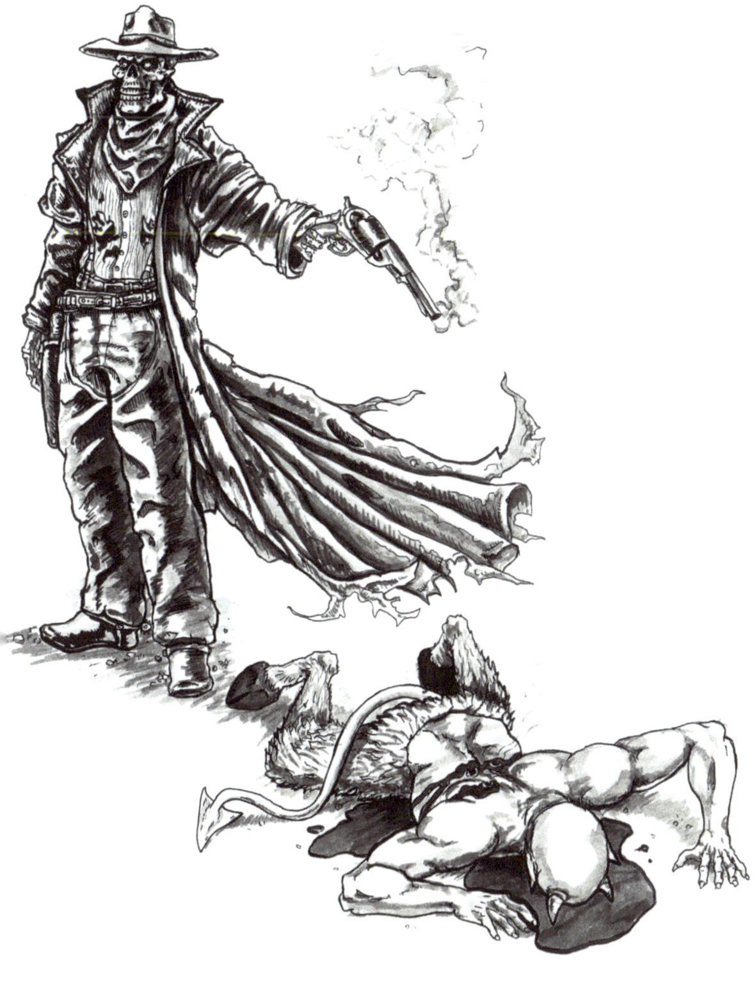

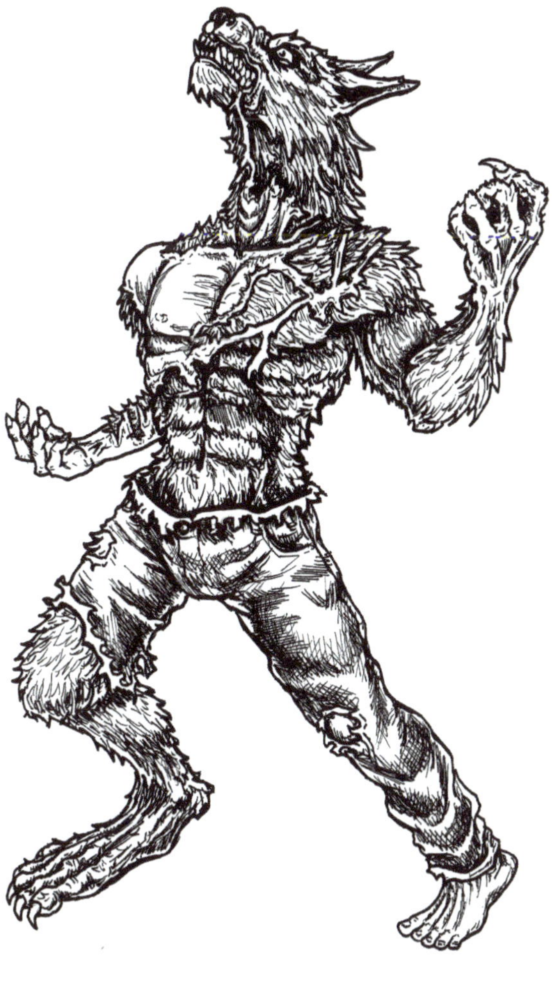

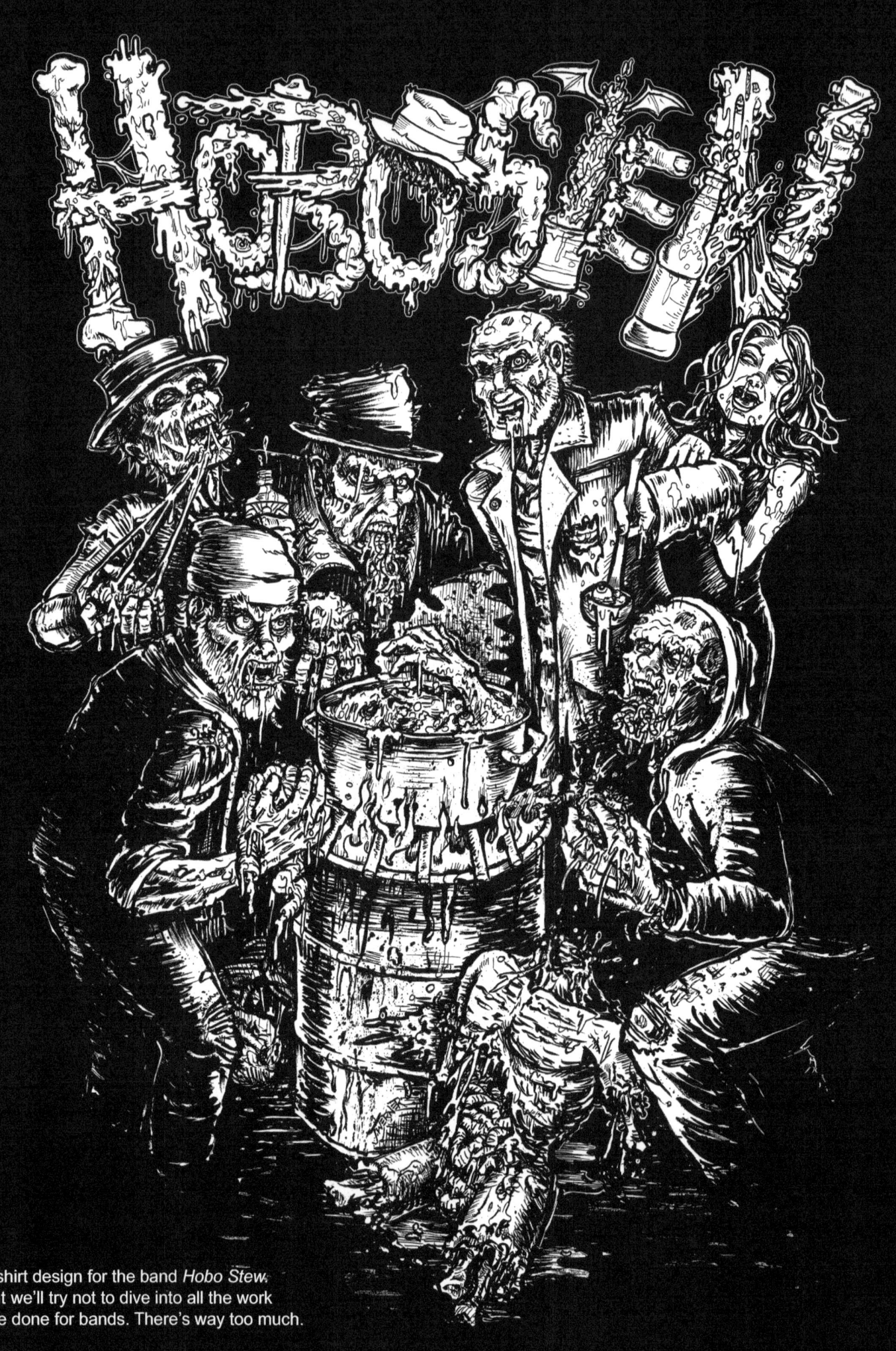

T-shirt design for the band *Hobo Stew*. But we'll try not to dive into all the work I've done for bands. There's way too much.

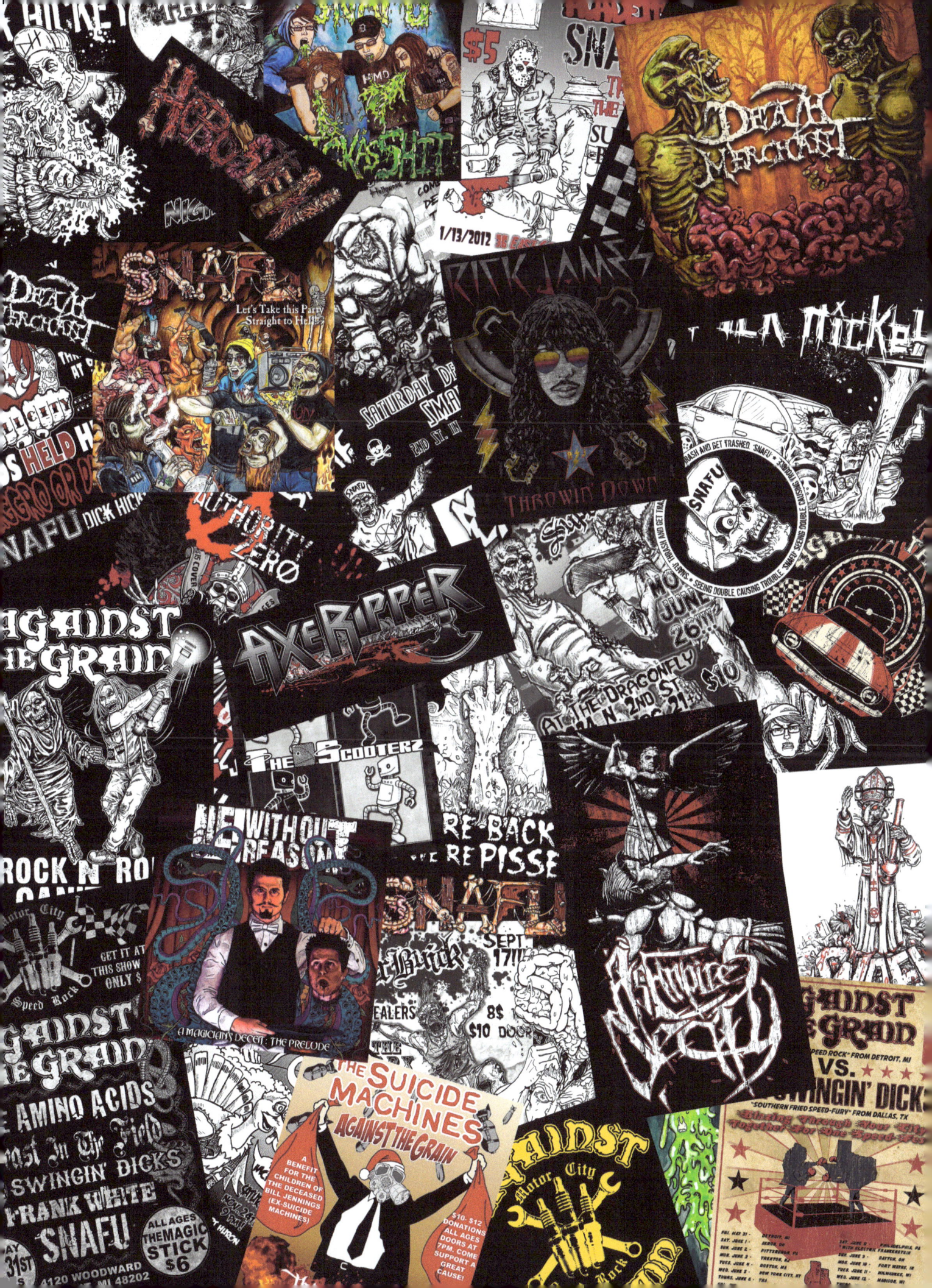

COLLECT THE WHOLE
MASTERS OF THE DARK ART SERIES AT
www.ASYLUMPUBLICATIONS.com

All characters and titles not in the public domain remain protected pursuant to the copyright owners or claimants of the respective studios, production companies, filmmakers, authors, or other rights holders, if applicable. The inclusion herein of such characters and titles is strictly for journalistic and/or informational commentary or scholarly review and use of the same is in no way intended to imply transfer, authorization, ownership, or other claimant rights other than for such use.

www.ingramcontent.com/pod-product-compliance
Lightning Source LLC
Chambersburg PA
CBHW040455220526
45473CB00004B/1643